DISNEYLAND HAS ALWAYS BEEN A SPECIAL PLACE FOR ME.

AFTER MY LAST TRIP THERE IT WILL MEAN MUCH MUCH MORE TO ME.

THIS BOOK IS GIVEN TO A DEAR FRIEND OF MINE WHO TRULY APPRECIATES LITTLE KNOWN FACTS"!.

ESPECIALLY THE ANSWER HIGHLIGHTED ON PAGE 27.

MERRY CHRISTMAS

Col M

DEC 1997

D0193366

The Ultimate
Disney Trivia Book

·······························

The Ultimate

Trivia Book

Kevin F. Neary and Dave Smith

HYPERION

New York

Library of Congress Cataloging-in-Publication Data

Neary, Kevin F.
The Ultimate Disney trivia book / by Kevin F. Neary and David R. Smith.
    p.   cm.
  ISBN 1-56282-925-4
  1. Walt Disney Company—Miscellanea. I. Smith, Dave. II. Walt Disney Company. III. Title.
NC1766.U52D516 1992
741.5′09794′93—dc20   92-23944
                                                         CIP

                        10 9 8 7 6

CONTENTS

·····················

Television

Disneyland

Walt Disney World

Magic Kingdom

Walt Disney World

EPCOT Center

Walt Disney World

Parks and Attractions

Walt Disney

FOREWORD

·················

What are the names of the Seven Dwarfs? Can you name Zorro's horse? Which young actor played the role of Jim Hawkins in *Treasure Island*? Which came first, *Fantasia* or *Pinocchio*?

No matter where we go, Disney trivia is part of our daily lives. Everyone grew up with Disney. If you ask most people what was the first movie they ever saw, the answer will probably be a Disney film. Personally, my earliest memories are of *Song of the South*. Bobby Driscoll, who starred in that film, was about my age, and I identified with him. I cried for him when he was gored by the bull, and I cheered when Uncle Remus helped give him the will to live. The Disney versions of the classics have become thoroughly ingrained in people all over the world, sometimes, however, to the displeasure of librarians and other academicians. But who can listen to Paul Dukas's *The Sorcerer's Apprentice* without picturing in their mind Mickey Mouse being overpowered by an army of water-carrying brooms? Who can read the Grimm Brothers' original fairy tale of "Snow White" and not smile at remembering Walt Disney's Dopey racing back through the house for one more good-bye kiss. Who can read P. L. Travers's charming book *Mary Poppins* and not visualize Julie Andrews cleaning up the kids' bedroom with a snap of her fingers.

Today's parents often had their earliest movie-going experiences when their parents took them to see the latest Disney animated feature. That earlier generation also can harbor fond memories of Saturday mornings spent in the local movie theater watching cavalcades of Disney cartoons, one after another, featuring Mickey Mouse, Donald Duck, Goofy, and Pluto. Sadly, those days have passed, taken over by economical limited animation on television aimed at keeping kids occupied on those Saturday mornings. But parents do have their memories. That fondness for the Disney films is passed on from generation to generation. It is not at all surprising that The Walt Disney Company caters to those memories by frequently rereleasing the animated classics in theaters and on video cassette, by publishing books and comics starring the Disney characters, by showing the great cartoons on The Disney Channel, by licensing merchandise featuring the Disney characters, and by building theme parks where families can experience their Disney memories brought into three-dimensional reality.

But it is not solely memories. The Disney classic films and characters have universal and timeless appeal. Kids growing up today can become just as fascinated by the latest Disney home video release of *Pinocchio* or *The Jungle Book* as their parents were. And, with video, we are seeing a new phenomenon. The kids are watching the films over and over and over. Often they learn the dialogue and songs by heart, and the Disney classics thus become part of their lives. Kids today are just as much in love with Mickey Mouse as were previous generations. Walt Disney was obviously a genius at knowing what the public wanted in the way of entertainment, and that is why his works have survived the test of time.

Back in 1970, The Walt Disney Company had the foresight to establish the Walt Disney Archives, and I was lucky enough to be the one chosen to start the collection. Now, twenty-two years later, the Archives is still proving its value to the company. Probably no other company in the world reuses its past as much as Disney, so there is constant need for the information in the Archives generated by departments throughout the organization. As the keeper of Disney history, it also naturally falls to us to be the keeper of Disney trivia. Many times in the past we have been called on to produce Disney trivia questions for licensed games, for in-house contests, for radio promotions, and for many other reasons. As the source for Disney facts, we are also relied on to proofread Disney trivia produced by others.

The Disney Stores were created in 1987 as a new merchandising concept within The Walt Disney Company. The Stores, located in selected shopping malls throughout the country, would bring Disney into the hinterlands. The Stores would be Disney-owned and operated, would carry Disney merchandise exclusively, and would mirror the Disney quality that is so apparent at Disneyland or Walt Disney World. But, the Stores brought an added attraction. There are avid Disney fans throughout the country, but many of them were able to get their oft-needed Disney fix only through their viewings of the latest Disney film or occasional visits to the Disney parks. Now there is a Disney Store in their neighborhood. Now they can get a job working for the company they love so much, without having to move to California or Florida.

As more and more avid Disney enthusiasts came on board, The Disney Store management had an idea: Let's run a Disney trivia competition for the store personnel. The cast members (Disney parlance for employees) from each store would work together to answer monthly lists of trivia questions. These would be graded, and then the highest-scoring stores would be invited to send representatives to district competitions each fall. From those district competitions, finalists would be chosen to represent their stores at a trivia showdown at Disneyland park in October. The Disney Stores turned to the Archives to prepare the questions for the competition, so for the past several years I have been challenged to come up with hundreds of stumpers for the knowledgeable Disney Store cast members.

The first competition was won by a representative of a store in Palo Alto, California, followed the next year by one in Dallas, Texas. In 1991 the cast member who won the trivia showdown was Kevin Neary, from The Disney Store in King of Prussia, Pennsylvania. Kevin, who amazed the audience at the finals with his knowledge of Disney trivia, had come upon a unique way of cramming for the competition. He decided to put together his own Disney trivia book. Working from his own Disney memories and from Disney reference sources available to him, Kevin came up with 999 Disney trivia questions. This trivia book is a result of Kevin's lifelong interest in Disney.

We have arranged the book by category. First you will find questions on The Fabulous Five (Mickey Mouse, Minnie Mouse, Donald Duck, Goofy, and Pluto), then ones on the short cartoons and featurettes, the animated features, the live-action films, Disney on television, the parks, and, finally, a general category on Walt Disney and his legacy. You will find historical questions, questions on plot, questions on characters, and even a few that you wouldn't be expected to know the answer to, but they were so much fun we thought you would enjoy them too.

Our Disney trivia book is not aimed just at Disney collectors. The questions and answers will help you learn more about Disney in all its forms, whether the animated films and characters, the live-action films, the parks, or other aspects of the Disney world. We meant them to be both fun and educational. The answers often give a little more information than asked for in the question, to make the book a learning experience as well. Fun little tidbits of information add interest to the book.

When I came to Disney in 1970, I had always been a fan of the Disney films. I had watched the Disney television shows and had persuaded my parents to take me to Disneyland shortly after it opened. But I was in no way a Disney expert. My first real work with Disney came when I, as a reference librarian at UCLA, decided to compile a Disney bibliography. The idea came to me soon after the shock of hearing of Walt Disney's death on December 15, 1966. When I discovered that no bibliography had ever been done, I contacted the Disney Studio to see if they would sanction my project and open files for me so I could obtain needed information. They were pleased to help, and for the next three years, I toiled on this bibliography in my spare time, gaining my first basic knowledge of Disney lore. This project is what put me in the right place at the right time when Disney decided it was time to start an Archives.

As soon as I established the Archives, I realized that I would have to become *the* Disney expert. Not only were staff members throughout the company coming to me for the answers, but I also got referrals from writers, newspapers reporters, television commentators, lawyers, students and others outside the company. For the first few years, I did not feel very confident with my answers, but slowly, the Disney history began to sink in. When you work with the Disney material day in and day out, some of it naturally rubs off. Besides, I would get the same questions over and over again. Before long, I could answer them without looking up the answer. So, over the past twenty-two years, without seriously striving for that label, I have become the "Disney expert." With this trivia book, I have found the chance to try on others some of those questions that are always being asked of me.

This Disney trivia book has been a labor of love on Kevin's and my part, and I hope you find that it brings back a lot of your Disney memories. It certainly did that for us while we were compiling it.

DAVE SMITH
Walt Disney Archives
September 1992

The Ultimate
Disney Trivia Book

·······························

Mickey Mouse

November 18, 1928

Questions

1. According to legend, when did Walt Disney create Mickey Mouse and what name did he first give him?
2. Who provided the original voice of Mickey Mouse, and when did he utter his first words?
3. What Disney artist is credited with animating the first Mickey Mouse cartoons?
4. What was the first merchandise item to feature Mickey Mouse?
5. In what year were the first Mickey Mouse Clubs formed?
6. When did the first Mickey Mouse comic strip appear?
7. In what year did the first Mickey Mouse watch appear and what was the name of the company that manufactured it?
8. Name the first color cartoon to feature Mickey Mouse and which was his last black and white cartoon?
9. Which three Disney full-length feature presentations were the only ones to include an animated Mickey Mouse?
10. In 1953 Mickey appeared in the cartoon *The Simple Things;* he didn't appear again in a theatrical release until 1983. What is the title of that film?

Mickey Mouse

····························

Answers

1. According to Walt Disney, the idea for Mickey Mouse came to him while traveling on a train from New York back to California. He had just lost his rights to Oswald the Lucky Rabbit and he came up with the idea for the mouse. He originally called him Mortimer, but his wife, Lillian, convinced him to change it to Mickey Mouse because it sounded cuter.

2. The original voice of Mickey Mouse was actually Walt Disney himself. In 1946 James Macdonald took over the job and he held it until 1983, when Wayne Allwine, the current voice took over. Mickey's first words were uttered in the 1929 cartoon, *The Karnival Kid.*

3. Ub Iwerks was asked by Walt Disney to animate the very first Mickey Mouse cartoons, a task he did almost single-handedly.

4. A child's school tablet in 1929.

5. The first Mickey Mouse Clubs were formed in 1929 in movie houses throughout the country.

6. The first Mickey Mouse comic strip was published on January 13, 1930. The strips were drawn by Ub Iwerks for a few weeks and then his assistant, Win Smith, drew them for three months, to be succeeded by Floyd Gottfredson, who continued to draw the strip for forty-five years.

7. The first Mickey Mouse wristwatch was produced by the Ingersoll-Waterbury company in 1933. The dial read: "Mickey Mouse Ingersoll," and it sold originally for $3.75, then $2.95.

8. The first Mickey Mouse color cartoon, *The Band Concert,* premiered on February 23, 1935. The last black and white Mickey Mouse cartoon was *Mickey's Kangaroo,* which actually premiered some two months after the first color one, on April 13, 1935.

9. *Fantasia* in 1940, *Fun and Fancy Free* in 1947, and *Who Framed Roger Rabbit* in 1988.

10. *Mickey's Christmas Carol.*

Minnie Mouse

· ·

November 18, 1928

Questions

1. What was the title of the very first cartoon in which Minnie Mouse appeared?
2. Who provided the voice of Minnie Mouse?
3. What does Minnie Mouse present to Mickey Mouse in the early cartoon, *Plane Crazy*?
4. In some cartoons Minnie Mouse has had a dog Pluto is absolutely crazy about. What was her name?
5. What was the name of Minnie Mouse's bird?
6. Were Mickey and Minnie ever married?
7. The early Minnie wore a hat with what on it?
8. What part does Minnie play in the 1938 cartoon, *Brave Little Tailor*?
9. What patriotic Revolutionary War character did Minnie Mouse portray on the merchandise available during the Bicentennial celebration in the Disney theme parks?
10. When did Minnie Mouse make her first full-length feature appearance?

Minnie Mouse

Answers

1. Minnie Mouse has always been there for Mickey and she premiered with him in *Steamboat Willie*.

2. The voice of Minnie Mouse was originally provided by women from the studio's ink and paint department. Marcellite Garner did it from 1930 through 1940. Thelma Boardman was the voice from 1940 through 1942, and then Ruth Clifford took over. Today, Russi Taylor provides the voice.

3. Minnie Mouse gives Mickey a lucky horseshoe.

4. Minnie's dog was the pretty little Pekinese Fifi. Fifi made her first appearance in the 1933 cartoon, *Puppy Love*.

5. Minnie had a bird named Frankie in the 1947 cartoon, *Figaro and Frankie*. Figaro was the popular cat from *Pinocchio*.

6. Matter of fact, Minnie and Mickey were married in the 1932 cartoon, *Mickey's Nightmare;* however, Pluto was there to save the day for Mickey, for when he licked his hand to wake him up, Mickey realized it was only a dream.

7. The early Minnie wore a hat with one flower on it.

8. Minnie played the role of the fair Princess Minnie; she, along with a reward of six million pazoozas was the prize for slaying the giant. Mickey was, of course, the victor and he was crowned "Royal High Killer of the Giant."

9. Minnie portrayed Betsy Ross.

10. Minnie Mouse, unlike Mickey Mouse, Donald Duck, and Goofy, never appeared in a full-length feature presentation until *Who Framed Roger Rabbit* in 1988.

Pluto

· · · · · · · · · · ·
1930

Questions

1. In what cartoon did Pluto make his first screen appearance?
2. When was Pluto first referred to as Pluto?
3. Pluto had another name prior to Pluto. What was that name?
4. In over sixty years as Mickey's faithful dog, Pluto has only uttered two words. What were they and when did he say them?
5. What was the title of Pluto's only Academy Award—winning cartoon?
6. In the classic 1939 cartoon, *Society Dog Show,* who does Pluto save from the fiery embers?
7. Who does Pluto encounter in the 1943 cartoon, *Private Pluto?*
8. What song does Pluto sing in the 1947 Academy Award—nominated *Pluto's Blue Note?*
9. Pluto has always been known for his way with the ladies. What is the name of Pluto's second great love?
10. In *Pluto's Judgement Day,* who puts Pluto on trial?

Pluto

·········

Answers

1. The first appearance of Pluto was the 1930 cartoon, *The Chain Gang* but he was without a name.
2. In the 1931 cartoon, *The Moose Hunt*.
3. He was called Rover in the 1930 cartoon, *The Picnic,* in which he was Minnie Mouse's dog.
4. The only two words ever uttered by Pluto were "Kiss me," from the 1931 cartoon, *The Moose Hunt.*
5. *Lend a Paw* (1941) won the Academy Award for Best Cartoon. It was actually a remake of the 1933 cartoon, *Mickey's Pal Pluto.*
6. In *Society Dog Show* we see Pluto rescuing his first great love, the Pekinese, Fifi.
7. Pluto encounters Chip an' Dale in the 1943 cartoon, *Private Pluto;* however, the two famous little chipmunks were still unnamed in their first screen appearance.
8. Pluto sings "You Belong to My Heart." This song appeared earlier in the 1945 feature presentation, *The Three Caballeros.*
9. Pluto's second great love was the dachshund, Dinah.
10. Pluto is tried by a jury of cats.

Goofy

1932

Questions

1. Who was the original voice for Goofy?
2. Most people don't realize that Goofy actually had other names prior to being called Goofy. What was his original name?
3. When did Goofy make his first screen appearance?
4. What was the name of the first cartoon that featured Goofy as the star?
5. Over the years Goofy was known for his "How To" series. Which one was the first in this series and who was the narrator?
6. What characters does Goofy portray in the 1950 cartoon on safe driving, *Motor Mania*?
7. Has Goofy ever appeared in any full-length feature presentations?
8. What name was given to Goofy in the theatrical cartoons featuring him as a harried father?
9. In comic stories, what was the name of the superhero version of Goofy?
10. What is the name of the television series featuring Goofy?

Goofy

·········

Answers

1. Pinto Colvig was originally the voice of Goofy. He also supplied the voices for Practical Pig in *Three Little Pigs* (1933) and Grumpy in *Snow White and the Seven Dwarfs* (1937) among others.

2. The original name of Goofy was "Dippy Dawg." He was later known as "Dippy the Goof."

3. Goofy, as Dippy Dawg, first appeared in the 1932 cartoon, *Mickey's Revue.*

4. Goofy had his first starring role in 1939, when he and his pet grasshopper, Wilbur, appeared in *Goofy and Wilbur.*

5. The first Goofy "How To" cartoon was *Goofy's Glider* in 1940, and the soon-to-be-familiar voice of the narrator was John McLeish.

6. Throughout the years Goofy appeared in several cartoons about safe driving. In the 1950 classic *Motor Mania,* Goofy played the roles of the mild-mannered Mr. Walker and the ferocious Mr. Wheeler.

7. Goofy has actually appeared in four full-length features: as an amateur horseman in *The Reluctant Dragon* in 1941; as El Gaucho Goofy in the 1943 feature, *Saludos Amigos;* as one of the starving farmers in the "Mickey and the Beanstalk" section of *Fun and Fancy Free* in 1947; and as a bit player in *Who Framed Roger Rabbit* in 1988.

8. Goofy was known as George Geef.

9. Goofy became Super Goof.

10. The 1992 series is *Goof Troop.*

Donald Duck

June 9, 1934

Questions

1. In what cartoon did Donald Duck make his screen debut?
2. Who supplied the original voice of Donald Duck?
3. What was the title of Donald Duck's Academy Award–winning cartoon?
4. Can you name Donald Duck's three nephews?
5. Can you name Daisy Duck's three nieces?
6. What is Donald Duck's full name?
7. What was the title of Donald Duck's United States government-backed cartoon encouraging individuals to pay their income taxes on time in order to help the war effort?
8. What was Donald Duck's first color cartoon?
9. What university uses Donald Duck as its mascot?
10. Has Donald Duck ever appeared in any Disney full-length feature presentations?

Donald Duck

. . . .

Answers

1. Donald Duck made his screen debut in a bit part in the 1934 Silly Symphony, *The Wise Little Hen.*

2. Clarence "Ducky" Nash, a radio personality, provided the original voice for the famous duck. Nash continued doing the voice for fifty years. He even came out of retirement in 1983 to supply Donald's voice in *Mickey's Christmas Carol.* After his death, animator Tony Anselmo took over.

3. Donald Duck's Academy Award—winner for Best Cartoon was *Der Fuehrer's Face* (1943). The original name for the cartoon was going to be *Donald Duck in Nutziland,* but because of the success of the song "Der Fuehrer's Face" by Oliver Wallace, the film's title was changed.

4. Huey, Dewey, and Louie made their screen debut in 1938 in *Donald's Nephews.* In the cartoon, Donald Duck's sister Dumbella sent him a postcard asking him if he could look out for them. Donald agreed and hasn't been able to get rid of them since.

5. Daisy Duck has three darling nieces named April, May, and June.

6. Donald Fauntleroy Duck. Donald's full name is shown on his draft notice in *Donald Gets Drafted.*

7. When the government asked Walt Disney why he used Donald Duck as the star for this government-backed cartoon, he replied that "Donald Duck is our equivalent to MGM's Clark Gable." The name of the film was *The New Spirit,* and the concept proved so successful that in 1943 a sequel was produced entitled *The Spirit of '43.*

8. Since Donald Duck's first apperance was in a Silly Symphony, *The Wise Little Hen* gave him the chance to appear in color before his colleagues. Mickey and Goofy didn't appear in their first color cartoon until *The Band Concert* in 1935. The Silly Symphonies had gone to color in 1932.

9. The University of Oregon is the only university allowed to use Donald Duck as its mascot.

10. Donald Duck holds the lead over his colleagues with six full-

length feature appearances: *The Reluctant Dragon* in 1941; *Saludos Amigos* in 1943; *The Three Caballeros* in 1945; the "Mickey and the Beanstalk" section of *Fun and Fancy Free* in 1947; *Melody Time* in 1948; and *Who Framed Roger Rabbit* in 1988.

Animated Cartoons and Featurettes

Questions

1. What was the title of the first Alice Comedy?
2. What is the name of the Long John Silver–type monstrous cat who is the longest-lasting Disney animated character?
3. In what cartoons did this monstrous cat make his first appearance and his most recent theatrical appearance?
4. Can you name the first Oswald the Lucky Rabbit cartoon?
5. In *Steamboat Willie* what punishment does the Captain give Mickey Mouse?
6. What popular hero from the 1920s does Mickey Mouse imitate in the 1928 cartoon *Plane Crazy*?
7. The cartoon *Mickey Follies* in 1929 is most notable for the appearance of Mickey's theme song. What is the name of that song?
8. What is Mickey Mouse's profession in the 1931 cartoon *Traffic Troubles*?
9. What are the names of the first and last Silly Symphonies?
10. What was the name of the first color Silly Symphony and where did it premiere?
11. Mickey's early pal, Horace, was easily recognizable by what item of wearing apparel?
12. What does Mickey Mouse dream he is doing in the 1933 cartoon *Mickey's Gala Premiere*?
13. Name the Three Little Pigs in the Academy Award–winning cartoon of 1933.
14. What is notable about the piano in *Three Little Pigs* (1933)?
15. What cartoon introduced the song "The World Owes Me a Living"?
16. What song from *The Grasshopper and the Ants* did Goofy adopt as his own theme song?
17. What character made his auspicious debut with the words, "Who? Me? Oh, no, I've got a bellyache"?

18. What two nursery rhymes does Donald Duck recite in 1934's *Orphan's Benefit*?
19. Which Mickey Mouse cartoon was censored by British officials in 1933 because it was viewed as frightening and "unsuitable for young children"?
20. Which two relatives of Mickey Mouse made their only screen appearance together in the 1934 cartoon *Mickey's Steamroller*?
21. What were the full names of the stars of the 1934 Academy Award—winning cartoon *The Tortoise and the Hare*?
22. What are the names of the two penguins featured in the 1934 cartoon *Peculiar Penguins*?
23. What character had the slogan, "Slow but sure"?
24. In the 1934 Silly Symphony *The Cookie Carnival*, the town of Cookie Town is looking for a new what?
25. Who killed Cock Robin in the cartoon *Who Killed Cock Robin?*, and what actress was used as a caricature for the part of Jenny Wren?
26. What character does Mickey Mouse portray in the 1933 cartoon *Mickey's Mellerdrammer*?
27. With whom does Mickey Mouse joust in the 1933 cartoon *Ye Olden Days* in order to win the hand of Minnie Mouse?
28. What date is considered Donald Duck's birthdate?
29. What character was constantly interrupting Mickey in the 1935 classic cartoon *The Band Concert,* and what song was he playing?
30. Name the three kittens that appear in the 1935 Academy Award—winning cartoon *Three Orphan Kittens.*
31. In 1935 Walt Disney himself directed *The Golden Touch,* a cartoon about what legendary king?
32. How do Mickey, Donald, and Goofy get in trouble in *Mickey's Service Station* (1935)?
33. In what cartoon does Mickey emulate Alice from a Lewis Carroll story?
34. Which players made up the two teams in the 1936 classic cartoon *Mickey's Polo Team*? (A hint: Each team had four members and one featured Hollywood stars and the other Disney cartoon characters.)
35. In *Mickey's Grand Opera* (1936), Donald Duck is teamed up with what operatic diva?
36. Disney made several Christmas cartoons but only one for Easter. What was its name?
37. Who was Mickey's rival, the one trying to win the heart of Minnie Mouse in the 1936 cartoon *Mickey's Rival*?

38. What were the names of the two mice featured in the Academy Award–winning cartoon *Country Cousin*?

39. What was Daisy Duck's original name, and when did she make her first screen appearance?

40. When did Daisy Duck first appear in a cartoon with the name Daisy?

41. What was the name of the Academy Award–winning cartoon in 1937, and why was this film so significant?

42. In *Clock Cleaners* (1937), Donald Duck throws one of his major temper tantrums when he tangles with what?

43. Which Disney cartoon won two Academy Awards, one for the cartoon itself and the other for the equipment used in making the cartoon?

44. Who places the phone call to Mickey's team of Ghost Exterminators in the 1937 cartoon *Lonesome Ghosts*?

45. In *Mr. Mouse Takes a Trip*, who does Mickey stuff into his suitcase?

46. In the classic cartoon *Symphony Hour*, what is the name of the greedy radio sponsor?

47. In *Donald's Cousin Gus*, what kind of animal is Gus?

48. What is the name of the famous bull featured in the 1938 Academy Award–winning cartoon?

49. In *Wynken, Blynken and Nod* (1938), what are the three boys fishing for?

50. Why is the Ugly Duckling different from the other ducklings?

51. When Mickey as the Brave Little Tailor brags about killing seven with one blow, what is he talking about?

52. What was the name and breed of dog who played Pluto's constant oppressor in cartoons of the 1940s?

53. Who tried to convince the perennially stupid Chicken Little that the sky was falling in the 1943 cartoon?

54. What character tried to protect the sheep in *The Legend of Coyote Rock* (1945)?

55. In what cartoon were Chip an' Dale first referred to by those names?

56. What song does Donald Duck sing after being hit over the head with a flower pot in the 1947 cartoon, *Donald's Dilemma*?

57. Who was Ajax?

58. Who was Dolores?

59. What kind of animals were Bent-Tail and Bent-Tail Junior?

60. What do Donald Duck, Daisy, and the three darling little nephews ride in the 1941 cartoon *The Nifty Nineties*?

61. What kind of animal was Marblehead in the 1946 cartoon *Lighthouse Keeping* starring Donald Duck?

62. What kind of animal was Salty in the 1947 cartoon *Rescue Dog* starring Pluto?

63. What kind of animal gives Mickey and Pluto trouble when they venture to Australia in the 1948 cartoon *Mickey Down Under*?

64. What was the name of the baby kangaroo that gave Donald Duck so much grief in the 1948 cartoon *Daddy Duck*?

65. What is the name of the brave engineer in the cartoon of that title from 1950?

66. What is the name of the cat who teams up with Pluto in the 1951 cartoon *Cold Turkey*?

67. The character Figaro, who first appeared in *Pinocchio* in 1940, became a star in his own right and starred in three cartoons. Can you name any of them?

68. What was the name of the large moose with tiny antlers who teamed up with Morris, the small moose with large antlers, in the 1950 cartoon *Morris, the Midget Moose*?

69. The wacky bear, Humphrey, made life difficult for what roly-poly forest ranger in several cartoons?

70. What was the first cartoon ever to be filmed in Cinema-Scope®?

71. What troublesome little pair climbed into the tree and made themselves right at home in the 1952 cartoon *Pluto's Christmas Tree*?

72. How does *Susie, the Little Blue Coupe* get saved from the junkyard?

73. What is the name of the famous sheepish lion, and who was the narrator of the Academy Award–nominated cartoon?

74. In the 1952 cartoon *Trick or Treat* starring Donald Duck and his nephews, we are introduced to a cheery witch and her broom. What are their names?

75. What was the title of the first 3-D cartoon?

76. Who are the two title characters in the 1953 cartoon *Ben and Me,* and who was the narrator of this entertaining featurette?

77. In what 1954 cartoon did guinea pigs multiply faster than a railroad station agent could manage them?

78. What is the name of Paul Bunyan's blue ox in the 1958 film *Paul Bunyan*?

79. What made Paul Bunyan different from the other woodsmen?

80. Which character tried to teach us *How to Have an Accident*

in the Home (1956) and *How to Have an Accident at Work* (1959)?

81. *Goliath II* was the first animated featurette to use Xerox processing for transferring the animators' pencil drawings to celluloid. What kind of animal was Goliath II?

82. What is Windwagon Smith's strange means of transportation in *The Saga of Windwagon Smith* (1961)?

83. Who provided the voice of Scrooge in his first Disney theatrical appearance in *Scrooge McDuck and Money* (1967)?

84. What famed comic-book artist is credited with creating the character of Uncle Scrooge?

85. What is the name of the character who sings the title song in the 1969 Academy Award—winning cartoon *It's Tough to Be a Bird*?

86. In 1978, a group of Finns censored Donald Duck comics. What didn't they like about his clothing?

87. In *Mickey's Christmas Carol,* what parts did Mickey Mouse, Donald Duck, and Goofy play in this animated version of Charles Dickens's story?

88. What two characters collect for the poor, and what part does J. Thaddeus Toad play in the 1983 featurette *Mickey's Christmas Carol*?

89. Who was the voice of Ebenezer Scrooge in *Mickey's Christmas Carol*?

90. Who portrayed the ghosts of Christmas Present, Past, and Future in *Mickey's Christmas Carol*?

91. Where do the Gummi Bears live, and who is their spell-casting leader?

92. Duke Igthorn and his ogres menace what princess in *The Gummi Bears*?

93. What is the mythical home of the Wuzzles called?

94. In the 1990 featurette *The Prince and the Pauper,* what are Mickey and Goofy trying to sell at the beginning of the film?

95. What is pictured on the Prince's ring in *The Prince and the Pauper*?

96. According to the Prince in *The Prince and the Pauper,* what are the only two expressions one in government had to remember to say?

97. What does Goofy lose on his way out the window in *The Prince and the Pauper*?

98. What part does Donald Duck play in *The Prince and the Pauper,* and who provided the voice?

99. Who piloted the helicopter and airplane in *DuckTales: The Movie, Treasure of the Lost Lamp*?

100. What criminal organization does Darkwing Duck fight against?

Animated Cartoons and Featurettes

1. The pilot film was *Alice's Wonderland* made in 1923; however, it was never publicly released. The first film released was *Alice's Day at Sea*.
2. The name of that villainous cat is Pegleg Pete, also known as Black Pete, Big Bad Pete, Bad Pete, or just Pete.
3. Pete made his first appearance in *Alice Solves the Puzzle* in 1925, and he appeared in *The Prince and the Pauper* as Captain Pete in 1990.
4. Oswald the Lucky Rabbit first appeared in *Trolley Troubles* in 1927.
5. Mickey is sent to the galley to peel potatoes, much to the delight of a parrot sitting and squawking in a porthole.
6. Mickey Mouse imitates aviator Charles Lindbergh.
7. "Minnie's Yoo Hoo," written by Carl Stalling, became Mickey's theme song beginning with *Mickey's Follies* in 1929.
8. Mickey Mouse played the role of a taxi driver in *Traffic Troubles*.
9. The first Silly Symphony was *The Skeleton Dance* of 1929, and the last was the 1939 Academy Award–winner, *The Ugly Duckling*.
10. The first color Silly Symphony was *Flowers and Trees,* which premiered on July 30, 1932, at Grauman's Chinese Theatre in Hollywood.
11. Horace Horsecollar wore, what else, an oversized horsecollar.
12. Mickey dreams that he is the guest of honor at the premiere of his latest film at Grauman's Chinese Theatre in Hollywood. In attendance are some of the silver screen's finest, including Clark Gable, Laurel and Hardy, Charlie Chaplin, and Mae West.
13. Fifer Pig, Fiddler Pig, and Practical Pig. The three famous pigs premiered on May 4, 1933, at Radio City Music Hall in New York City.
14. It is made of bricks, just like Practical Pig's house.

15. The 1934 Silly Symphony *The Grasshopper and the Ants* featured Pinto Colvig, better known for being the voice of Goofy, singing the catchy little song "The World Owes Me a Living."
16. Goofy used "The World Owes Me a Living" as his theme song.
17. Trying to get out of doing some work, Donald Duck uttered these words in *The Wise Little Hen.*
18. The two nursery rhymes are "Mary Had a Little Lamb" and "Little Boy Blue."
19. The British censored Mickey's *The Mad Doctor.*
20. Mickey's nephews Morty and Ferdy (sometimes spelled Ferdie).
21. Max Hare and Toby Tortoise.
22. The two penguins are named Polly and Peter.
23. The plodding tortoise, Toby, used the motto "Slow but sure" to beat the cocky Max Hare in *The Tortoise and the Hare.*
24. Cookie Town was looking for a new Cookie Queen to crown.
25. Cock Robin wasn't killed but rather just wounded by Dan Cupid's arrow. The character Jenny Wren was a caricature of actress Mae West.
26. Mickey Mouse played the role of Uncle Tom from *Uncle Tom's Cabin.*
27. Mickey jousts with Dippy Dawg, who plays a prince, in this 1933 short.
28. June 9, 1934, is regarded as Donald Duck's birthdate; that was the release date of *The Wise Little Hen,* the first cartoon in which he appeared.
29. Donald Duck is constantly interrupting Mickey by playing "Turkey in the Straw" while Mickey is conducting "The William Tell Overture."
30. The three little orphan kittens are Tuffy, Fluffy, and Muffy.
31. Walt Disney directed the story about King Midas, but he wasn't happy with the results, so he never directed another cartoon himself.
32. They manage to demolish Pete's car when he brings it in just because of a squeak.
33. Just like Alice, Mickey goes *Thru the Mirror* in this 1936 cartoon.
34. The Disney team includes Mickey Mouse, Donald Duck, Goofy, and the Big Bad Wolf. The team of Hollywood stars features Oliver Hardy, Stan Laurel, Charlie Chaplin, and Harpo Marx. Who actually won they never really said.
35. Almost overflowing the balcony is the buxom Clara Cluck.
36. The only Easter cartoon was *Funny Little Bunnies* (1934).

37. Mickey's annoying rival was Mortimer. Ironically, Walt Disney had originally proposed Mortimer as Mickey's name.
38. Abner was the country mouse and Monty was the city mouse.
39. Daisy's original name was Donna Duck in the 1937 cartoon *Don Donald*.
40. It wasn't until *Mr. Duck Steps Out* in 1940 that Daisy was actually referred to by that name.
41. The 1937 Academy Award–winner was *The Old Mill*. This was the first release utilizing the multiplane camera, a device that helped create a three-dimensional look to cartoons.
42. Donald tangles with the mainspring of the huge clock.
43. *The Old Mill* (1937) won awards for itself and the multiplane camera.
44. Mickey, Donald, and Goofy are invited to rid the spooky mansion of its ghosts. What the three do not realize is that the invitation has been extended by the ghosts themselves.
45. Mickey stuffs Pluto into his luggage so conductor Pete will not observe him bringing a dog on board the train. All Mickey wants to do is get from Burbank to Pomona.
46. The greedy radio sponsor looked a lot like Pete, but his name was Mr. Sylvester Macaroni.
47. Donald's gluttonous cousin is a goose.
48. Ferdinand was the flower-sniffing bull featured in *Ferdinand the Bull*. In the cartoon Walt Disney is caricatured as the matador.
49. Wynken, Blynken, and Nod are fishing for golden stars as they sail through the night sky in their wooden boat. The impressive effects in the film were made possible by the Disney Studio's newly invented multiplane camera.
50. The Ugly Duckling is really a swan.
51. Even though the townspeople think Mickey killed seven giants with one blow, he really meant that he swatted seven flies with his fly swatter.
52. It seemed that no matter where Pluto turned, there was Butch the bulldog to impede his progress.
53. Foxey Loxey hoped his ruse would bring Chicken Little and the others to become his dinner.
54. The intrepid Pluto was on guard at the sheep pen.
55. The first time the two famous chipmunks had their present names was in the cartoon appropriately titled *Chip an' Dale* in 1947.
56. Donald Duck is heard singing "When You Wish Upon a Star," the Academy Award–winner from *Pinocchio* (1940).
57. Ajax was an escaped gorilla from the 1944 cartoon *Donald*

Duck and the Gorilla.

58. Dolores was an elephant who appeared in several shorts with Donald and Goofy.

59. Bent-Tail and Bent-Tail Junior were a father-and-son coyote team.

60. Donald Duck, Daisy, and the three darling nephews were riding a bicycle built for five.

61. Marblehead was a pelican.

62. Salty was a seal.

63. Mickey and Pluto encounter Esther the emu.

64. The baby kangaroo was named Joey.

65. The brave engineer was Casey Jones, and Jerry Colonna provided the narration.

66. Milton was the cat who teamed up with Pluto.

67. Figaro starred in *Figaro and Cleo* (1943), *Bath Day* (1946), and *Figaro and Frankie* (1947).

68. Balsam was the large moose with tiny antlers. When Morris perched on his head, they made a fine pair.

69. The ranger was J. Audubon Woodlore, who worked at Brownstone National Park.

70. The first cartoon in CinemaScope was *Toot, Whistle, Plunk and Boom* (1953), which also won an Academy Award.

71. Chip and Dale made themselves right at home in *Pluto's Christmas Tree* of 1952.

72. She is bought by a teenager for $12.50; he rebuilds her and soon has her feeling young again.

73. Lambert from *Lambert, The Sheepish Lion* (1952), and the narrator was Sterling Holloway.

74. We are introduced to Witch Hazel and her broom, Beelzebub.

75. *Adventures in Music: Melody* was the first and *Working for Peanuts* was the second and last Disney 3-D cartoon; both were produced in 1953.

76. The two stars were Benjamin Franklin and a church mouse named Amos. The narrator was once again Sterling Holloway, whose distinctive voice became quite familiar to Disney fans over the years. He was the voice of the stork in *Dumbo* (1941), the Cheshire Cat in *Alice in Wonderland* (1951), Kaa the snake in *The Jungle Book* (1967), and Winnie the Pooh, just to name a few.

77. *Pigs is Pigs.*

78. Paul Bunyan's blue ox was named affectionately "Babe."

79. Paul Bunyan was gigantic: "63 ax handles high."

80. It wasn't Goofy, whom we usually think of as the bungler, but rather Donald Duck.

81. No, Goliath II wasn't a gorilla; he was a small elephant.
82. Windwagon creates a sailing ship out of a Conestoga wagon, which is propelled across the desert by the wind.
83. The original voice of Uncle Scrooge was Bill Thompson, a voice that became quite a standard in Disney films. He also did the voice of Mr. Smee from *Peter Pan* (1953) and some of the dogs in *Lady and the Tramp* (1955).
84. Carl Barks created Uncle Scrooge for a Donald Duck comic book, and soon the miserly character had his own series. Scrooge was much better known through the comic books than from his rare film appearances.
85. The character was known as M.C. Bird.
86. They were shocked that Donald Duck doesn't wear pants.
87. Mickey Mouse played the role of Bob Cratchit, Donald Duck the part of Uncle Ebenezer's nephew Fred, and Goofy portrayed Scrooge's former business partner Jacob Marley.
88. Rat and Mole are collecting for the poor, and J. Thaddeus Toad plays the role of Fezzywig, Scrooge's old boss. All three first appeared in the feature *The Adventures of Ichabod and Mr. Toad* (1949).
89. Alan Young, who earlier had been the star of television's "Mr. Ed," was Ebenezer Scrooge.
90. The Ghost of Christmas Present was Willie the Giant from the feature *Fun and Fancy Free* (1947). The Ghost of Christmas Past was Jiminy Cricket from *Pinocchio* (1940). The Ghost of Christmas Future was Disney's longest-running character, the villainous Pete.
91. The Gummi Bears live in Gummi Glen in the Kingdom of Dunwyn, and their spell-casting leader is Zummi Gummi.
92. Princess Calla and her friend the page Cavin often have to outwit Igthorn with the help of the Gummi Bears.
93. The Wuzzles live in The Land of Wuz.
94. Mickey is trying to sell kindling for firewood, and Goofy, having no success at all, is trying to sell snowcones.
95. The picture on the Prince's ring is of the royal crown.
96. According to the Prince, the only two phrases someone in government has to know are: "That's a splendid idea, I'm glad I thought of it" and "Guards, seize him!"
97. Goofy loses his red polka-dot shorts going out the window.
98. Donald plays the Prince's valet, and Tony Anselmo was the voice.
99. Launchpad McQuack is the fearless pilot.
100. Darkwing Duck fights against the Fiendish Organization for World Larceny, or F.O.W.L. for short.

Snow White and the Seven Dwarfs

December 21, 1937

Questions

1. Name the song Snow White sings at the wishing well.
2. The Wicked Queen is extremely jealous of Snow White's beauty and instructs whom to kill her?
3. Can you name all of the Seven Dwarfs?
4. Which one of the Dwarfs has white eyebrows, which one wears glasses, and which one is bothered by a fly?
5. Can Dopey talk?

6. Who was the young girl who provided the voice for Snow White?

7. Who helps Snow White clean the cottage? (Hint: This same group also summons the Dwarfs from the diamond mine when Snow White is in trouble.)

8. What type of pie does Snow White offer to bake and what type of flower is Sneezy allergic to?

9. Which Dwarf does not have a beard?

10. Which Dwarf refuses to wash up for dinner?

11. How does the Wicked Queen address her mirror when she wants to find out who is the fairest one of all?

12. How does the Queen convince Snow White to eat the apple?

13. According to the Queen's spell, what is the only way in which Snow White can be saved after tasting the apple?

14. How do the Dwarfs manage to dispose of the witch after they discover what she has done to Snow White?

15. What 1939 film broke the record held by *Snow White and the Seven Dwarfs* as the top-grossing film?

Snow White and the Seven Dwarfs

Answers

1. The song is "I'm Wishing."
2. The Queen instructs her huntsman, Humbert, to kill the Princess, but he cannot bring himself to hurt Snow White, so instead he brings the Queen the heart of a pig.
3. Here's an easy way to remember the famous seven by following this rule: two D's, two S's, and three emotions. Therefore: Doc and Dopey; Sleepy and Sneezy; and Bashful, Happy, and Grumpy.
4. Happy has the white eyebrows; Doc is the one who wears glasses; and Sleepy is bothered by a fly.
5. Well, when asked by Snow White if Dopey could talk Happy said, "He don't know, he never tried!"
6. Adriana Caselotti.
7. The woodland animals help Snow White clean the cottage, as well as summon the Dwarfs when she is in trouble.
8. Snow White offers to bake gooseberry pies, and Sneezy is allergic to goldenrod.
9. Dopey is the one without a beard.
10. Grumpy, so the other Dwarfs have to grab him and see that he washes.
11. The Queen would say, "Magic mirror on the wall."
12. The Queen, disguised as an old woman, convinces Snow White that it is a magic wishing apple, one bite and all of her dreams would come true.
13. Only "love's first kiss" can save Snow White.
14. They chase her up a rocky mountain, and she falls to her death when part of a cliff gives way.
15. *Gone With the Wind.*

Pinocchio

······················

February 7, 1940

Questions

1. In one of the opening sequences we see the wood-carver Geppetto looking out the window and wishing upon a star. What did Geppetto wish for?
2. Much to Geppetto's surprise his wish is granted. Who grants this wish?
3. What are the names of Geppetto's pet fish and cat?
4. In order to become a real boy, what three qualities does Pinocchio have to demonstrate?
5. What is Pinocchio sent off with on his first day of school?
6. Who manages to sell Pinocchio to the evil showman Stromboli?
7. What is the name of the fox's awkward companion?
8. What song does Pinocchio sing at Stromboli's puppet show?
9. What does Stromboli threaten to do with Pinocchio if he does not do as he says?
10. What happens to Pinocchio when he tells lies in Stromboli's wagon?
11. After Pinocchio escapes from Stromboli he is again thrown into even more trouble with the Coachman. Where does the Coachman take Pinocchio and what happens to little boys there?
12. What is the name of the monstrous whale that Pinocchio discovers has swallowed Geppetto?
13. How do Pinocchio and the others manage to get out of the inside of the whale?
14. What is the name of the Academy Award—winning song from this feature, and who wrote it?
15. At the conclusion of the feature, Jiminy Cricket is presented with a medallion; what words are written on it?

28

Pinocchio

·················

1. Geppetto wishes that Pinocchio would become a real little boy.
2. The Blue Fairy comes to grant Geppetto's wish.
3. Geppetto's fish is named Cleo and his cat is Figaro. Figaro later went on to star in cartoons of his own.
4. In order to become a real little boy, the Blue Fairy states that Pinocchio must be "brave, truthful, and unselfish."
5. Pinocchio is sent off to school with a book and an apple.
6. Pinocchio is sold to Stromboli by the fox whose full name is J. Worthington Foulfellow, but he's usually known as Honest John.
7. The cat is named Gideon.
8. "I've Got No Strings."
9. Stromboli threatens to chop Pinocchio into firewood.
10. His nose grows longer with each lie he tells.
11. Pinocchio is taken to Pleasure Island, from which little boys never return as little boys but are turned into donkeys and sold to work in salt mines.
12. The name of the whale is Monstro.
13. They build a smoky fire and make him sneeze.
14. The famous song is "When You Wish Upon a Star," performed by Jiminy Cricket as voiced by Cliff Edwards and written by Ned Washington and Leigh Harline.
15. The medallion is given to Jiminy Cricket by the Blue Fairy and it reads: "18k Gold Official Conscience."

Fantasia

November 13, 1940

Questions

1. In what theatre did *Fantasia* have its world premiere?
2. What famous orchestra and conductor were used for the feature?
3. What was the name given to the unique sound system used for *Fantasia*?
4. What is the first thing seen in the film?
5. According to the narrator, what three types of music will the audience experience in *Fantasia*?
6. What piece of music constitutes the first musical segment?
7. The second musical segment is from Tchaikovsky's *Nutcracker Suite*. What is the name Disney gave to the small mushroom featured in the "Chinese Dance" section?
8. In the *Nutcracker Suite,* what kind of creatures bring on autumn colors to the trees and later touch them with frost as winter comes?
9. What creatures do we see performing the "Arabian Dance" from the *Nutcracker Suite*?
10. The third musical segment is from Dukas's *The Sorcerer's Apprentice.* What is the name of the Sorcerer?
11. What does Mickey Mouse, the eager apprentice, borrow in order to make the magic work, and what went wrong?
12. What implement did Mickey Mouse use to try to stop the broom?
13. Who congratulate each other at the conclusion of the third musical segment?
14. The fourth musical segment is from Igor Stravinsky's "Rite of Spring." What two prehistoric creatures are locked in mortal combat?
15. The fifth musical segment is from Beethoven's "Pastoral Symphony." What is the setting?
16. What is the name of the mythological god who hurls lightning bolts down on Bacchus in the "Pastoral Symphony" segment?
17. Who supplies this Greek god with the thunderbolts he needs?
18. What is the name of Bacchus's donkey-unicorn?

19. Bacchus is the Greek god of what?
20. A dazzling image of what Greek god is represented as the sun in the "Pastoral Symphony"?
21. Who is the Greek goddess who shoots her arrow to create the stars in the night sky?
22. Which mythological flying horse can be seen in the "Pastoral Symphony"?
23. In the sixth musical segment, Ponchielli's "Dance of the Hours," what four types of animals are featured as the ballet dancers?
24. In the "Night on Bald Mountain" segment, what is the name of the demon?
25. What chased the demon back to where he came from?
26. In "Night on Bald Mountain," how does the demon disappear at the end of the film?
27. What religious song provides the counterpoint to "Night on Bald Mountain" to conclude *Fantasia*?
28. What radio personality appeared as the narrator of *Fantasia*?
29. What was the working title for *Fantasia*?
30. For what limited period did The Walt Disney Company make the *Fantasia* video cassette available for sale?

Fantasia

Answers

1. *Fantasia* had its world premiere at the Broadway Theatre in New York City. The theater, formerly called the Colony Theatre, was the same one in which Mickey Mouse's first cartoon, *Steamboat Willie* had opened on November 18, 1928, just twelve years earlier.

2. The orchestra was the Philadelphia Orchestra, conducted by Leopold Stokowski.

3. The unique sound system was called Fantasound, an early version of stereophonic sound.

4. The first thing the viewer sees are the silhouettes of the musicians entering and warming up.

5. The three types of music are: (1) music that tells a story; (2) music that has no plot but presents a series of pictures; and (3) music that exists for its own sake.

6. The first musical segment is Bach's Toccata and Fugue in D Minor.

7. The small mushroom is known as Hop Low.

8. Fairies work their wonders in helping with the change of seasons.

9. Fish with billowing tails.

10. The name of the Sorcerer is Yen Sid; now spell it backwards!

11. Mickey Mouse as the Sorcerer's Apprentice borrows the Sorcerer's hat to practice magic. But Mickey discovers magic can get out of hand, as the broom delivers more water than he expected.

12. Mickey tried to chop the boom up with a hatchet, but all he succeeded in doing was creating a lot more brooms.

13. Mickey Mouse runs up to conductor Leopold Stokowski and the two shake hands and congratulate each other.

14. The two creatures are a Tyrannosaurus Rex and a Stegosaurus.

15. The setting for the "Pastoral Symphony" is Mount Olympus.

16. Zeus is the god throwing lightning bolts at Bacchus.

17. Vulcan.

18. The name of Bacchus's donkey-unicorn is Jacchus.

19. The god of wine.

20. The god Apollo is featured as the sun in the "Pastoral Symphony," driving his fiery chariot.
21. Diana shoots the arrow, after Morpheus, the god of night, spreads his cloak over the landscape.
22. The mythological flying horse is Pegasus.
23. The four animals are the ostriches with their leader Mlle. Upanova; elephants with Elephanchine; hippopotami with the lovable Hyacinth Hippo; and alligators led by Ben Ali Gator.
24. The name of the demon is Chernabog.
25. The demon is chased back by the first sign of light and the ringing of the church bells.
26. He folds his wings around himself and turns into the mountain.
27. Franz Schubert's "Ave Maria."
28. The narrator of *Fantasia* was Deems Taylor, radio personality of the Metropolitan Opera.
29. *The Concert Feature.*
30. The sale was announced for fifty days only, and then it was to be removed from sale to make way for an eventual sequel to *Fantasia*.

Dumbo

October 23, 1941

Questions

1. At the beginning of the film we see an aerial view of the United States and then we zero in on one state that is the winter home of the circus. Which state is it?
2. Who delivers the baby elephant to his mother, and what famous Disney actor speaks the part?
3. What was the baby elephant originally going to be called by his mother?
4. Who gave Dumbo his famous name?
5. Why is Dumbo's mother locked away from her baby?
6. After the baby elephant's mother is locked away, who befriends Dumbo?
7. Because of his funny appearance, what job is Dumbo given in the circus?
8. After accidentally indulging in a bucket of spirits, what do Dumbo and his new friend think they see while hallucinating?
9. After his hallucinations, where does Dumbo wake up the next morning?
10. In the film we are introduced to a band of delightful crows. What song do they sing to Dumbo and his friend?
11. When Timothy wants Dumbo to fly, what object becomes a "magic" talisman to give him confidence?
12. In one of the final sequences of the film, Dumbo's ears are insured. How much are those ears insured for?
13. What was the name of the 1941 Academy Award–nominated song from Dumbo?
14. In what two other Disney-produced films did Dumbo the Elephant appear in some way?
15. How many words does Dumbo speak in the film?

Dumbo

1. Florida is the winter home for the circus.
2. The baby is delivered by Mr. Stork, whose voice was provided by Sterling Holloway.
3. Dumbo's mother was Mrs. Jumbo, and she was going to call her little one Jumbo Jr.
4. Dumbo was given his famous name by the four snooty elephants who shared the railroad car with Mrs. Jumbo; their names were Prissy, Catty, Matriarch, and Giggles.
5. One day Dumbo is being teased because of his unusual ears by a little boy. Mrs. Jumbo objects and tries to stop the boy, but circus personnel think she's going mad and lock her up.
6. Dumbo is befriended by Timothy Q. Mouse.
7. Dumbo becomes part of a clown act.
8. Dumbo and Timothy see "Pink Elephants on Parade."
9. Dumbo awakens perched high in a tree.
10. The five crows sing "When I See an Elephant Fly." The voice of the crow leader was Cliff Edwards, who sang "When You Wish Upon a Star" as Jiminy Cricket in *Pinocchio* in 1940.
11. Timothy presents Dumbo with a "magic feather."
12. Dumbo's ears are insured for $1,000,000.
13. The Academy Award–nominated song was "Baby Mine," written by Frank Churchill and Ned Washington.
14. Dumbo appeared in the 1986 feature *The Great Mouse Detective* as a toy in the toymaker's workshop, and in the 1988 film *Who Framed Roger Rabbit*, where he works for peanuts for R. K. Maroon.
15. Dumbo never speaks.

Bambi

August 13, 1942

Questions

1. What famous author wrote the book on which *Bambi* is based?
2. What event is heralded by the animals at the beginning of the film?
3. What do the animals in the forest call Bambi?
4. What is Bambi's first word, and who teaches him to talk?
5. What peculiar trait gives Thumper his name?
6. In one of the opening sequences we are introduced to Bambi's girlfriend. Can you name her?
7. What type of animal is Flower, and how did he get his name?
8. In what month does Bambi experience his first rain, thunder, and lightning?
9. How does Thumper describe the frozen water in the lake?
10. What traumatic experience does Bambi have as he races with his mother from the meadow?
11. What does "twitterpated" mean?
12. What caused the great fire in the forest?
13. At the end of the film, what does Flower name his first child?
14. How many children does Bambi have?
15. What do we see Bambi and his father doing in the final sequence of the film?

Bambi

Answers

1. Felix Salten.
2. The birth of the fawn, Bambi.
3. Bambi was called The Young Prince.
4. Thumper helped teach Bambi to talk, and his first word was "bird."
5. Thumper liked to thump his rear foot.
6. Bambi's girlfriend is Faline.
7. Bambi had just learned to speak when he came across a little skunk in a patch of flowers, and he naturally thought he was also a flower. The little skunk welcomed the name.
8. April, as the chorus sings "Little April Shower."
9. Thumper calls it "stiff," and he teaches Bambi to skate.
10. Bambi's mother is killed by hunters.
11. "Twitterpated" means to have fallen in love; and Friend Owl tells Bambi, Thumper, and Flower that one day they could become "twitterpated."
12. According to Bambi's father, the fire was started because "man was in the forest." Man's campfire started the fire.
13. Bambi, after his friend.
14. Bambi and Faline have twins.
15. At the end of the film we see Bambi and his father on top of a cliff; in a symbolic gesture Bambi's father leaves, signifying that Bambi is now the new Great Prince of the Forest.

Saludos Amigos

February 6, 1943

Questions

1. Why did Walt Disney go to South America in order to make this film?
2. *Saludos Amigos* was actually a combination of four different animated cartoons joined together to make up one full feature. In the first of these cartoons we see Donald Duck as a tourist at what Peruvian lake?
3. We are then introduced to Pedro. What is Pedro and what important task must he accomplish?
4. Why is Pedro suddenly given this important task?
5. Pedro is terrorized by what?
6. The next segment is "El Gaucho Goofy"; we see Goofy demonstrating something. What is Goofy attempting to demonstrate in this cartoon?
7. The final sequence is "Aquarela do Brasil." Who are the two main stars?
8. What famous beach is visited by the stars of "Aquarela do Brasil"?
9. Donald Duck's Brazilian friend is what kind of bird?
10. What clever device was used to tie the four sequences together to give them a more unified feel?

Saludos Amigos

Answers

1. To promote goodwill. The South American trip was suggested to Walt Disney by Jock Whitney, director of the motion-picture division for the Coordinator of Inter-American Affairs at the State Department.
2. Donald Duck is trying to be a tourist at Lake Titicaca.
3. Pedro happens to be a baby airplane who has suddenly been commissioned to carry the mail.
4. The reason why Pedro is suddenly given this important task is because his parents are ill. Papa Plane has a "cold in his cylinder-head" and Mama Plane has "high oil-pressure."
5. Aconcagua, one of the Andean mountains, which he encounters when trying to fly from Argentina to Chile.
6. Goofy is trying to demonstrate the differences between an American cowboy and an Argentine gaucho.
7. The two stars of "Aquarela do Brasil" are Donald Duck and Joe Carioca.
8. They visit Copacabana Beach in Rio de Janeiro.
9. Joe Carioca is a parrot.
10. The sequences were tied together very cleverly with live-action footage from Walt Disney's South American tour. Much of the footage was taken by Walt Disney himself, with a 16mm camera.

The Three Caballeros

February 3, 1945

Questions

1. In the opening sequence Donald Duck is celebrating his birthday. What is the date?
2. What four presents does Donald Duck receive from his South American relatives?
3. *The Three Caballeros* is like *Saludos Amigos* in that it ties together a collection of animated shorts to make one full feature. In the first of these cartoons we are introduced to Pablo. What type of animal is Pablo, and where does he want to go?
4. When Pablo's iceboat melts, what does he use as a makeshift boat?
5. What is the name of Pablo's stove?
6. What is so unusual about Gauchito's burro?
7. Gauchito is involved in a horse race. What is the prize?
8. Next we are welcomed by an old friend from *Saludos Amigos*. What is his name, and where do he and Donald go on their journey?
9. In one of the final sequences we are introduced to a new character, and the adventure then takes us to Mexico City. What is this new character's name?
10. Donald Duck, who was always known for being rather romantic and a lady-killer, falls in love, this time with two ladies in Mexico City. Can you name them?

The Three Caballeros

Answers

1. The date is Friday the 13th; however, Disney now uses June 9, 1934, as Donald's official birthday, the date when he first appeared in a film, *The Wise Little Hen*.
2. A movie projector and film, picture books, a piñata, and a flying serape.
3. Pablo is a penguin. However, Pablo is no ordinary penguin; he's the world's only cold-blooded penguin, and his goal is to leave the South Pole and head toward a warmer locale.
4. He presses his bathtub into service.
5. Pablo refers to his stove as "Smokey Joe."
6. This burro can fly.
7. The top prize for winning is 1,000 pesos.
8. Remember Joe Carioca from the "Aquarela do Brasil" section of *Saludos Amigos*? This time he and his friend Donald Duck are off to Baia, Brazil.
9. The new character is Panchito, a Mexican charro rooster. Donald Duck, Joe Carioca, and Panchito are The Three Caballeros.
10. While in Mexico City, Donald Duck falls in love with singer Dora Luz and dancer Carmen Molina. This is after he has already fallen in love with singer Aurora Miranda while in Baia.

Make Mine Music

August 15, 1946

Questions

1. *Make Mine Music* used the basic formula from *Fantasia* and gave it a modern and contemporary theme. One segment that was planned but dropped from *Fantasia* is used in *Make Mine Music*. Can you name that segment?
2. What were the names of the two lovers who helped end the long-standing hillbilly feud between the Martins and the Coys?
3. For what team did Casey play in the "Casey at the Bat" section?
4. What popular comedian provided the musical recitation for "Casey at the Bat"?
5. What did Casey do that brought him shame?
6. What popular band leader provided the music for "All the Cats Join In" and "After You've Gone"?
7. What famous pair of hats were immortalized by the Andrews Sisters?
8. What popular Disney voice personality was the narrator of Prokofiev's famous "Peter and the Wolf"?
9. With the characters in "Peter and the Wolf" being represented by musical instruments, what instrument represents Peter's grandfather?
10. In "Peter and the Wolf," what were the names of the little bird, the duck, and cat?
11. Who are the three feared hunters in "Peter and the Wolf"?
12. In what country is "Peter and the Wolf" set?
13. Who provided the musical voice behind Willie in "The Whale Who Wanted to Sing at the Met"?
14. Why does Professor Tetti Tatti want to harpoon Willie?
15. What happens to Willie at the end?

Make Mine Music

1. The section that appears in *Make Mine Music* is "Blue Bayou," using animation originally intended to accompany Debussy's "Clair de Lune."
2. The two lovers are Grace Martin and Henry Coy.
3. Casey played for the Mudville Nine.
4. The musical recitation for "Casey at the Bat" was by Jerry Colonna.
5. He struck out, ending the game with his team losing.
6. The two jazz numbers featured Benny Goodman and his band.
7. Johnny Fedora and Alice Bluebonnet.
8. The familiar voice of Sterling Holloway was used.
9. The bassoon.
10. The little bird's name was Sasha; the duck was known as Sonia; and Ivan was the cat.
11. Mischa, Yascha, and Vladimir.
12. Russia.
13. Nelson Eddy was the musical voice behind Willie the operatic whale (and all the other voices in the cartoon as well).
14. He thinks Willie has swallowed an opera singer, and the professor wants to save him. When Willie "auditions," singing three parts at once, the professor then thinks Willie has swallowed three opera singers.
15. He is harpooned and goes to heaven, where he is at last seen as a heavenly chorus.

Fun and Fancy Free

September 27, 1947

Questions

1. What popular Disney animated character introduces the "Bongo" section, and what song does he sing?
2. What popular vocalist sang and narrated the "Bongo" section?
3. What is the name of the female bear who befriends Bongo, and what is the name of her jealous suitor?
4. According to the story, how do bears show their affection for one another?
5. What method of transportation does Bongo use when he runs away from the circus?
6. What famous author wrote the story on which the "Bongo" sequence was based?
7. Who provided the voice of Mickey in the "Mickey and the Beanstalk" sequence?
8. In "Mickey and the Beanstalk," what is the name of the giant?
9. Billy Gilbert, known for his ferocious sneezing, provided the voice for the giant. What other Disney character is he known for voicing?
10. What does Mickey trade for the magic beans in "Mickey and the Beanstalk"?
11. What enables the magic beans to grow?
12. What do Mickey and the gang attempt to rescue from the giant in "Mickey and the Beanstalk"?
13. How do Mickey and his friends vanquish the giant?
14. What popular ventriloquist appeared in the live-action sequence and helped tie together the two animated sections?
15. When the "Mickey and the Beanstalk" segment aired on television in the 1960s, who was substituted as the narrator?

Melody Time

1. The famous cowboy who appeared in the live-action sequence was Roy Rogers.
2. Freddy Martin with Jack Fina at the piano.
3. Joyce Kilmer's "Trees."
4. New York Harbor was the setting for the "Little Toot" cartoon.
5. The Andrews Sisters made an encore performance in a Disney feature and performed the music for the "Little Toot" section.
6. He saves a huge ship that is foundering in a fierce storm.
7. Johnny Appleseed.
8. "Blame it on Samba" once again featured the popular stars from *Saludos Amigos* and *The Three Caballeros:* Donald Duck and Joe Carioca.
9. "Blue Shadows on the Trail."
10. The woman who captured the heart of Pecos Bill was Slue Foot Sue. Sue is lost when she tries to ride Pecos's horse, Widowmaker, and falls off on her bustle, which bounces her higher and higher until she lands on the moon and that's where she stays.

The Adventures of
Ichabod and Mr. Toad

October 5, 1949

Questions

1. Narrators play an important part in the presentation of these two featurettes. Who provided the narration for the "Ichabod" and "Mr. Toad" segments?
2. Who wrote the well-known story on which the Ichabod segment was based?
3. The character Ichabod Crane came to Sleepy Hollow, New York, to do what?
4. What does the Headless Horseman throw at Ichabod?
5. According to the story, when does the Headless Horseman lose his power?
6. Ichabod Crane and Brom Bones were trying to woo the daughter of the rich Baltus Van Tassel. What was her name, and which one of them did she eventually marry?

7. The "Mr. Toad" segment was based on what famous story?
8. When we first encounter J. Thaddeus Toad, Esq., we see him riding in a gypsy cart. Where is he going?
9. Where does Mr. Toad live?
10. What are the names of Mr. Toad's horse, his two loyal friends, and his accountant?
11. Why is Mr. Toad arrested?
12. What does Mr. Toad trade for the motor car?
13. Who helps Mr. Toad escape from jail?
14. Who is the bartender and leader of the weasels, and why does Mr. Toad wish he'd never met this individual?
15. When Mr. Toad's friends think they have cured him of his manias at the end of the film, what new sport does he take up?

The Adventures of Ichabod and Mr. Toad

Answers

1. The talents of Bing Crosby and Basil Rathbone were used.
2. Washington Irving wrote *The Legend of Sleepy Hollow*.
3. Ichabod Crane was a schoolmaster, and came to teach.
4. A Halloween pumpkin.
5. The Headless Horseman loses his power when he crosses the bridge leading out of Sleepy Hollow.
6. Baltus Van Tassel's daughter's name is Katrina, and Brom Bones eventually marries her (and daddy's money).
7. *The Wind in the Willows* by Kenneth Grahame.
8. According to the song, Mr. Toad is headed "nowhere in particular."
9. Mr. Toad lives in Toad Hall.
10. Mr. Toad's horse is named Cyril Proudbottom; his two loyal friends are Rat and Mole, and his accountant is Angus MacBadger.
11. Toad is arrested for apparently stealing a motor car.
12. The deed to Toad Hall.
13. His horse, Cyril Proudbottom, disguises himself as Toad's grandmother.
14. The bartender and leader of the weasels is Winky, who falsely accuses Mr. Toad of trying to sell him a stolen motor car.
15. Mr. Toad takes up flying, with a new airplane.

Cinderella

February 15, 1950

Questions

1. According to the song, what is a dream?
2. What are the names of Cinderella's two ugly stepsisters and her stepmother?
3. Who informs Cinderella that a mouse is trapped in a cage, and what does she name him?
4. Instead of "surprise" what does Gus say when the mice and birds present Cinderella with the gown they made for her?
5. Why couldn't Cinderella go to the ball in the gown made for her by the mice and birds?
6. What famous words does Cinderella's Fairy Godmother use in her spells?
7. What does Cinderella's Fairy Godmother use to create the carriage, the driver, the four horses, and the footman?
8. What time does the spell wear off according to the Fairy Godmother?

9. When the Fairy Godmother's magic spell ends, what are the only objects that do not transform back to their original form?
10. Why did the King instruct the Grand Duke to have the ball?
11. What prominent television personality provided the singing voice for Prince Charming?
12. Who brings the glass slipper for all the maids in the kingdom to try on?
13. Who climbs the stairs to save Cinderella from the locked room?
14. How does the stepmother attempt to stop Cinderella from trying on the glass slipper?
15. How does Cinderella prove that she was the one they were searching for?

Cinderella

1. According to the song, "A Dream is a Wish Your Heart Makes."
2. Cinderella's ugly stepsisters are Drizella and Anastasia; the stepmother is Lady Tremaine.
3. Jaq the mouse informs Cinderella that a new mouse is trapped in a cage. Cinderella rescues the scared little mouse, provides him with clothes, and names him Octavius, but she calls him Gus for short.
4. "Happy birthday."
5. The stepsisters tore it apart in a fit of spite.
6. The words "Bibbidi-Bobbidi-Boo."
7. The Fairy Godmother uses a pumpkin for the carriage, recruits Major the horse as the driver, turns the mice into the four horses, and Bruno the dog becomes the footman.
8. Cinderella must return by the last stroke of midnight.
9. A pair of glass slippers.
10. The King feared that his only son would remain unmarried, and the royal bloodline would end.
11. Mike Douglas.
12. The Grand Duke.
13. Jaq, Gus, and the dog Bruno.
14. She trips the Grand Duke's lackey, and the slipper shatters on the floor.
15. She has the matching slipper in her pocket.

Alice in Wonderland

July 28, 1951

Questions

1. Who wrote the popular book on which the film was based?
2. When we first encounter Alice what is she doing, and whom does she follow to start her on her journey?
3. What odd character helps Alice get through the keyhole?
4. Who are the twins who tell Alice the story of "The Walrus and the Carpenter"?
5. What is the song Alice sings with a group of flowers?
6. Alice is introduced to two crazy characters who invite her to their tea party. Name them and the actors who provided their voices.
7. Since the Mad Hatter has not removed the price tag from his hat, we know how much it cost. What was the price?

8. The mad tea party is actually a celebration party. What are these two screwball characters celebrating?
9. What is the substance that the Mad Hatter will not put in the White Rabbit's watch, declaring, "Don't let's be silly!"?
10. What is the title of the caterpillar's song?
11. At first, Alice thinks the Queen can help her get back home, but the Queen has other ideas. What is the Queen's declaration?
12. To what game does the Queen of Hearts challenge Alice?
13. In the film there are two cats, Alice's and another one who is always getting Alice into trouble. Can you name these two cats?
14. At the conclusion, when Alice wakes up under a tree, what does she realize?
15. Kathryn Beaumont, who provided the voice for Alice, later did the voice for what other Disney character?

Alice in Wonderland

1. Lewis Carroll.
2. Alice's sister is reading a history lesson to her. Alice then falls asleep. Her adventure begins when she sees the White Rabbit, and follows him.
3. The Doorknob assists Alice.
4. Tweedledee and Tweedledum tell the story of "The Walrus and the Carpenter."
5. "All in the Golden Afternoon."
6. The two crazy characters are the Mad Hatter and the March Hare, and their voices were provided by Ed Wynn and Jerry Colonna.
7. The tag reads 10/6, or ten shillings, sixpence.
8. The two zany characters are having an "unbirthday party," and, according to the Mad Hatter, "there are 364 'unbirthdays' in a year and only one birthday."
9. Mustard; of course this is after he has poured every other substance on the table into the watch.
10. The song is "A-E-I-O-U."
11. "Off with her head."
12. Croquet, but the Queen cheats.
13. They are Alice's own cat, Dinah, and the mischievous Cheshire Cat.
14. Alice realizes that all of her adventures have been a dream.
15. Wendy in *Peter Pan* (1953).

Peter Pan

February 5, 1953

Questions

1. Who wrote the play on which the Disney film was based?
2. George and Mary Darling had three children. Can you name them and tell where they live?
3. Who is the children's nursemaid?
4. Why does Peter Pan show up at the Darling house?
5. Why does Tinker Bell become so jealous?
6. What does Peter Pan sprinkle on the children to help enable them to fly?
7. Which is the way to Never Land, and at what time did Peter Pan and the children set out on their journey?
8. What item does the youngest Darling boy carry with him to Never Land?
9. Captain Hook and his accomplice, Mr. Smee, kidnapped the Indian Princess. What was her name, and where did they take her?
10. Which of Captain Hook's hands does the hook replace?
11. Why was a crocodile always following Captain Hook, and what warns the Captain of his approach?
12. Where is Peter Pan's hideout?
13. What element from the stage play, used to revive the dying Tinker Bell, was not used in the Disney version?
14. How does Peter Pan get everybody back to London?
15. Margaret Kerry was the live model for Tinker Bell, despite many rumors that the character had actually been patterned after what actress?

Peter Pan

Answers

1. Sir James M. Barrie.
2. Wendy, John, and Michael Darling, who live with their parents in Bloomsbury, a suburb of London.
3. She is a dog, named Nana.
4. Peter Pan comes to retrieve his shadow. He had previously come to listen to the stories.
5. Tinker Bell is jealous of Peter Pan's and Wendy's new friendship.
6. Some of Tinker Bell's pixie dust.
7. Never Land is located "second star to the right and straight on 'til morning," and Peter Pan and the three Darling children set out at 8:00 P.M.
8. Michael Darling carries a teddy bear.
9. Tiger Lily was taken by Captain Hook and Mr. Smee to Skull Rock.
10. Captain Hook's hook is on his left arm.
11. The crocodile had tasted him once by eating his hand, and wants another bite. Fortunately for the Captain, however, the crocodile swallowed a clock, and the ticking always gives him away.
12. At Hangman's Tree.
13. Having the audience clap if they believed in fairies.
14. Peter Pan has the pirate ship covered with pixie dust and uses it for transport.
15. Marilyn Monroe.

Sleeping

Questions

1. Name the three good fairies i
   colors do they wear?
2. What gifts were bestowed upon
   fairies?
3. Who is miffed because she was
   of the birth of the princess?
4. According to Maleficent, what
   finger on before the sun sets o
5. Where does Maleficent live?
6. Who were the fathers of the Pr
7. What did the three fairies renar
   was her real name?
8. Who does Maleficent use as her
9. After the Princess falls into he
   Maleficent surround the castle?
10. What was the name of Prince F
11. When Prince Phillip was being
    they threw rocks, shot arrows,
    did the three good fairies chan
12. How did the fairies refer to the
    sented to Prince Phillip when I
    cent?
13. In what form did Maleficent tr
    fight Prince Phillip?
14. The music for the film was ada
    music by what famous compose
15. What other major project was
    Walt Disney working on that
    slowed down production
    on *Sleeping Beauty*?

Lady and the Tramp

Questions

1. At the beginning of the feature, we see a quote by Josh Billings that reads, "Money can buy most things but it can't buy _____."?
2. The feature opens and closes during the same time of year. When is this?
3. What is the name of the bloodhound Trusty's grandfather?
4. According to the Scottish terrier, Jock, what has Trusty lost?
5. What were the names of Lady's owners?
6. Tramp convinces Lady that she will not be "top dog" around the household anymore when what event happens?
7. When Lady's owners had to take a trip, whom did they ask to mind the baby, and whom did she bring along with her?
8. Tramp is known by many different names. What is the name Tony and Joe call him, and what is Tramp's nickname for Lady?
9. What is the song with which Tony and Joe serenade Lady and Tramp while they are enjoying their plate of spaghetti at Tony's Restaurant?
10. What is the tune Peg sings to Lady at the dog pound, and what famous singer provided her voice?
11. The dogs howl a plaintive rendition of what song in the dog pound?
12. From what danger does Tramp save the baby?
13. When the careening dogcatcher's wagon is toppled over, who is crushed by it?
14. How many puppies did Lady and Tramp have, and whom do they resemble?
15. What photographic process was used for the first time in an animated feature by Walt Disney for this film?

Lady and [

Answers

1. "the wag of a dog's tail."
2. The story begins and ends a
3. Trusty's grandfather's name
4. Trusty has lost his sense of
5. Lady's owners were called J
6. When Jim Dear and Darling
7. Aunt Sarah came to mind th
   Siamese cats, Si and Am.
8. Tony and Joe called him "But
   refer to Lady as "Pigeon" or
9. "Bella Notte."
10. "He's a Tramp," co-authorec
    provided the voice of Peg as
11. "Home Sweet Home."
12. Tramp saves the baby from
    baby's room.
13. Trusty, but he only suffers a
14. Lady and Tramp have four pu
    mother and one little Tramp
    Scamp).
15. CinemaScope, a wide-screen p

Sleeping Beauty

Answers

1. Flora wore reds, Fauna was partial to green, and Merry-weather preferred blue.
2. Flora presented the young Princess the gift of "beauty." Fauna bestowed the gift of "song," and Merryweather changed Maleficent's evil spell around, so instead of the Princess dying, she would merely be asleep until awakened by "love's first kiss."
3. Maleficent, an evil fairy.
4. "Before the sun sets on her sixteenth birthday, she shall prick her finger on the spindle of a spinning wheel and die."
5. The Forbidden Mountains.
6. The Princess's father was King Stefan, and Prince Phillip's father was King Hubert. They wanted their children to marry so their kingdoms could be united.
7. The good fairies renamed the Princess Briar Rose when they took her to the woodcutter's cottage. The Princess's real name was Aurora. She was named after the dawn because she brought sunshine into the hearts of her parents.
8. First she sends out her goons to find Aurora, then her pet raven.
9. A forest of thorns.
10. Samson.
11. The rocks were transformed into bubbles, the arrows turned into flowers, and the boiling oil into a rainbow.
12. The sword was known as the Sword of Truth and the shield as the enchanted Shield of Virtue, and Prince Phillip used both to fight Maleficent.
13. An enormous fire-breathing dragon.
14. Composer George Bruns adapted his score from Tchaikovsky's famous ballet.
15. Disneyland Park, which opened in July 1955. His new television shows also took increasing amounts of his time.

One Hundred and One Dalmatians

January 25, 1961

Questions

1. Where did Roger and Anita first meet, and what is Roger's profession?
2. How did Anita Radcliff actually know Cruella De Vil?
3. Why did the evil Cruella want the puppies?
4. What does Cruella De Vil carry in her right hand?
5. While Roger and Anita were getting married in the church, what were Pongo and Perdita doing outside?
6. What is so notable about Cruella De Vil's hair?
7. How many puppies were actually born to Pongo and Perdita?
8. What was the name of the house Cruella De Vil owned in Suffolk?

9. What were the names of Cruella De Vil's hired hands, the ones who kidnapped the Dalmatian puppies?

10. In addition to Pongo and Perdita's puppies, how many other Dalmatian puppies were found at Cruella De Vil's estate?

11. Who was the Dalmatian puppies' favorite television star, and what dog food product was sponsor of his show?

12. Which one of the puppies was always hungry, and which one was particularly fascinated by the television?

13. What kind of animals were the Captain, Sergeant Tibs, and the Colonel, and how did they know Pongo and Perdita needed help?

14. How do the Dalmatians manage to disguise themselves as Labradors?

15. When Roger and Anita get all 101 dogs, Roger writes a song about what place with a rhyming name that they might have in the country?

One Hundred and One Dalmatians

Answers

1. Roger and Anita, with the help of Pongo, met in the park. Roger is an aspiring songwriter.
2. Anita and Cruella De Vil had been schoolmates.
3. Cruella wanted the puppies so she could make a fur coat out of them.
4. Cruella's trademark, the long cigarette holder.
5. Pongo and Perdita were getting "married" outside the church.
6. Half is black and half is white.
7. Pongo and Perdita had fifteen puppies.
8. Cruella De Vil's home was known as "Hell Hall."
9. Jasper and Horace Badun.
10. Eighty-four (84 + Pongo + Perdita + their 15 puppies = 101).
11. The star was Thunderbolt, and his show was sponsored by Kanine Krunchies.
12. The puppy Rolly was the one who was always hungry, and Lucky was especially fascinated by the television.
13. The Captain was a horse, Sergeant Tibs was a cat, and the Colonel was a sheepdog. They knew Pongo and Perdita needed help because of the "Twilight Bark."
14. They cover themselves with soot.
15. "Dalmatian Plantation."

The Sword in the Stone

December 25, 1963

Questions

1. What author wrote the book on which this film was based?
2. In what country is the film set?
3. Who was the narrator?
4. What was the inscription on the stone that held the sword?
5. What very inept animal was stalking Wart during the film?
6. Before being introduced to Merlin, Wart, or Arthur, was an aspiring squire for whom?
7. How does Merlin go through history?
8. What is the name of Merlin's very talkative and highly educated pet owl?
9. What three different things does Merlin change Arthur into to teach him the lessons of life?
10. With whom does Merlin have the Wizards' Duel, and what are the rules?
11. How does Merlin eventually win the Wizards' Duel?
12. In the middle of the movie Merlin takes off into the future. Where does he go?
13. Why did Wart need the sword that he found in the stone?
14. What does Wart have to do to prove to the disbelievers that he actually pulled the sword from the stone?
15. According to Merlin, what are "the two most important things in life"?

The Sword in the Stone

Answers

1. T. H. White.
2. England, in the sixth century.
3. Sebastian Cabot provided the narration. He later went on to provide the voice of Bagheera the panther in *The Jungle Book* (1967), and was the first narrator of the Winnie the Pooh films.
4. "Whoso pulleth out this sword of this stone and anvil is right-wise king born of England."
5. A wolf.
6. Wart had been an aspiring squire for Sir Kay.
7. Merlin actually goes through history "in reverse."
8. Archimedes.
9. A fish, then a squirrel, and then a little bird.
10. Merlin faces Mad Madam Mim in the Wizards' Duel. The rules are: "Rule one: No mineral or vegetable, only animal; Rule two: No make-believe things like pink dragons and stuff; Rule three: No disappearing; Rule four: No cheating." Well, needless to say, Mad Madam Mim did cheat, but Merlin still was victorious.
11. Merlin transforms himself into a germ and infects Mim.
12. Merlin takes off to twentieth-century Bermuda.
13. He had forgotten to bring Sir Kay's sword to the tournament.
14. He has to pull the sword from the stone all over again.
15. "Knowledge and wisdom."

The Jungle Book

October 18, 1967

1. The man cub Mowgli was abandoned at birth. Who raised him?
2. Who was the leader of the wolf pack, and where did they conduct their meetings?
3. What famous personalities provided the voices for Kaa the Snake, Bagheera, and Baloo?
4. Louie, the King of the Apes, wanted what from Mowgli?
5. Who sings "I Wanna Be Like You"?
6. Where in the jungle did King Louie live?
7. When Baloo puts on a disguise, what does he use for a mouth?
8. Who was the leader of the army of elephants, and what does he call his troop?
9. According to the song, what did Baloo want to teach Mowgli?
10. How does Kaa try to get Mowgli under his power?
11. Who sings "Trust in Me"?
12. Who were Buzzie, Dizzy, Flaps, and Ziggy?
13. What did Shere Khan fear most?
14. Which character comes back to life after having apparently been slain by Shere Khan?
15. Who gets Mowgli to leave the jungle for the man village?

The Jungle Book

Answers

1. Rama and his family of wolves adopted the man cub Mowgli.
2. Akela was the leader, and they met at Council Rock.
3. Sterling Holloway was the voice of Kaa the Snake, Sebastian Cabot was the voice of Bagheera, and Disney newcomer Phil Harris provided the voice of the jungle bum Baloo.
4. Louie wants Mowgli to teach him the secret of "man's red fire."
5. King Louie, voiced by Louis Prima, sings it to Mowgli.
6. King Louie lived in the Ancient Ruins.
7. Coconut shells.
8. Colonel Hathi was the leader of the Dawn Patrol.
9. "The Bare Necessities." The song was nominated for an Academy Award.
10. He tries hypnotizing him.
11. Kaa the Snake sings it to Mowgli.
12. Four vultures.
13. Fire.
14. Baloo. He revives during Bagheera's funeral oration.
15. A young girl.

The Aristocats

December 24, 1970

Questions

1. What famous French singer was coaxed out of retirement to sing the title song?
2. Who provided the voice for Thomas O'Malley, the alley cat?
3. What is O'Malley's full name?
4. Can you name Duchess's three kittens?
5. Which one of the kittens was musically inclined, and which one was the artist?
6. What were the names of the two geese who were on their way to Paris to meet their Uncle Waldo?
7. What famous Disney actor did the voice of Roquefort the mouse?
8. A fortune was going to be left to Duchess and her kittens by whom?
9. When the butler drugs the cats and takes them off to the country, what method of transportation does he use?
10. Who are the two dogs and horse who help rescue the cats?
11. Besides Scat Cat, what four nationalities are represented among his feline singing group?
12. What was the name of the butler who attempted to dispose of Duchess and her three kittens so he could collect the inheritance?
13. To what distant place does the butler plan to ship the cats in a trunk?
14. What happens to the butler after he is attacked by all of the cats?
15. What kind gesture is done by Duchess's owner at the conclusion of the film?

The Aristocats

1. Maurice Chevalier came out of retirement because of his respect for Walt Disney.
2. Phil Harris was the voice of Thomas O'Malley, the alley cat. Phil Harris had been the voice of Baloo in *The Jungle Book* three years before.
3. Abraham de Lacy Giuseppe Casey Thomas O'Malley.
4. Marie, Berlioz, and Toulouse.
5. Berlioz was the musician, and the artist was Toulouse.
6. Abigail and Amelia Gabble.
7. Sterling Holloway.
8. Madame Bonfamille was going to leave her inheritance to Duchess and her three kittens upon her passing.
9. A motorcycle with a sidecar.
10. The two dogs were Napoleon and Lafayette, and the horse was Frou-Frou.
11. Chinese Cat, English Cat, Italian Cat, and Russian Cat.
12. Edgar was the butler who would collect the entire inheritance if Duchess and her kittens could somehow be eliminated from the picture.
13. To Timbuktoo.
14. Edgar is pushed into the trunk that was meant to dispose of the cats and is carted away instead.
15. Madame Bonfamille decides to convert her home into a place where all the stray cats in Paris could find refuge.

Robin Hood

November 8, 1973

1. What did Robin Hood and Little John dress up as to fool the Prince out of the tax money and jewels?
2. What was unusual about the picture Maid Marian had of Robin Hood?
3. Roger Miller supplied the voice of the rooster who was also the narrator. What was this character's name?
4. What was the reward for the capture of Robin Hood?
5. What did Robin Hood give to Skippy the rabbit for his birthday?
6. What was the name of Prince John's snake?
7. What was the name of Skippy's turtle friend?
8. What was the prize for winning the archery tournament, who were the two finalists, and what disguise did Robin Hood wear in the event?
9. At the archery tournament, how did the snake plan to get a bird's eye view of the proceedings and hopefully capture Robin Hood?
10. Which one of "The Merry Men" did Robin Hood and Little John rescue from being hanged at the Nottingham prison?
11. What type of animals are the Nottingham prison guards, Nutsy and Trigger?
12. Little John, in disguise at the archery tournament, gives Prince John what nickname?
13. What kind of animal is the Sheriff of Nottingham?
14. What bad habit does Prince John demonstrate whenever someone mentions his mother?
15. What kind of animals are Prince John and King Richard?

Robin Hood

1. They disguised themselves as two gypsy women fortune-tellers willing to tell the Prince's future.
2. It was actually a "wanted" poster.
3. The character was Allan-a-Dale.
4. The reward for Robin Hood's capture was 10,000 ingots.
5. A bow and arrow and his very own Robin Hood–style hat.
6. Sir Hiss.
7. Toby.
8. The top prize was a "golden arrow" and a kiss from the fair Maid Marian. The two finalists were, of course, Robin Hood, who came disguised as a stork from Devonshire, and the Sheriff of Nottingham.
9. He floated up to the sky inside a balloon.
10. Friar Tuck.
11. Two vultures.
12. PJ.
13. The Sheriff is a wolf.
14. He sucks his thumb.
15. They are both lions, though King Richard is a majestic king-of-the-jungle type, while Prince John is kind of scrawny.

The Many Adventures of Winnie the Pooh

March 11, 1977

Questions

1. *The Many Adventures of Winnie the Pooh* is actually a combination of three Winnie the Pooh featurettes linked together, along with a bit of new animation, to make one full feature. Can you name the three Winnie the Pooh featurettes?
2. What famous author wrote the original stories about Winnie the Pooh?
3. Who were the voices of Winnie the Pooh and Tigger?
4. Where do Christopher Robin and his friends play?
5. What is the name on the sign over the door of Winnie the Pooh's house?
6. What is the name of Kanga's little boy?
7. When Pooh uses a balloon to float up to a bees' nest in a tall tree, what does he try to convince the bees that he is?
8. Where does Winnie the Pooh get stuck, and how long does he have to remain there?
9. What is Tigger's annoying trait?

10. According to Tigger's song, what is the most wonderful thing about Tiggers?
11. What weird creatures try to steal Pooh's honey during a nightmare?
12. What is the name of Piglet's grandfather?
13. Whose house is destroyed during a blustery day?
14. During a blustery day, which character becomes a "kite" as his scarf unravels?
15. Which character does not appear in the original book and is "ding-dang glad of it"?

The Many Adventures
of Winnie the Pooh

Answers

1. *Winnie the Pooh and the Honey Tree* (1966); *Winnie the Pooh and the Blustery Day* (1968); and *Winnie the Pooh and Tigger Too* (1974).
2. A. A. Milne.
3. Paul Winchell supplied the voice of Tigger, Sterling Holloway was Winnie the Pooh, and Sebastian Cabot was the narrator.
4. In the Hundred Acre Wood.
5. The sign reads "Mr. Sanders."
6. Roo.
7. Having rolled in the mud, he tells the bees he is a little black rain cloud.
8. Winnie the Pooh first gets stuck in Rabbit's house because he ate too much honey, and he'll have to remain there until he gets thin again. Then he gets stuck in the honey tree, where presumably he will be content to stay as long as the supply of honey holds out.
9. He is constantly bouncing.
10. The most wonderful thing about Tiggers is that he's the "only one."
11. Heffalumps and Woozles.
12. Trespassers Will.
13. Owl's house is destroyed, prompting Eeyore to volunteer to find a new one for him.
14. Piglet.
15. Gopher.

The Rescuers

June 22, 1977

Questions

1. What was the name of Madame Medusa's shop?
2. How did word get to Bernard and Bianca that Penny was in danger?
3. Who was the philosophical old cat who helped lead Bernard and Bianca to Penny?
4. Where does Orville take Bernard and Bianca?
5. Bernard and Bianca work with what organization, and where is its headquarters?
6. What position did Bernard originally hold at this organization?
7. Orville is the owner of what business?
8. Who provided the voices of Madame Medusa, Bernard, and Bianca?
9. In an effort to catch Madame Medusa, Bernard and Bianca catch a ride with a dragonfly. What is its name?
10. What is the name of Madame Medusa's bumbling accomplice?
11. Medusa's two evil henchmen are what kind of animal?
12. What is the name of the jewel Medusa is searching for?
13. Where does Medusa hide the jewel after Penny has obtained it for her?
14. What does Penny eventually do with the jewel that Madame Medusa is searching for?
15. What is the name of the Academy Award–nominated song from *The Rescuers*?

The Rescuers

1. Madame Medusa's Pawn Shop Boutique.
2. A message in a bottle that floated into New York Harbor read: "To Morningside Orphanage, New York. I am in terrible, terrible trouble. Hurry. Help!—Penny"
3. Rufus.
4. To Devil's Bayou.
5. The International Rescue Aid Society has its headquarters in the basement of the United Nations Building in New York.
6. Janitor.
7. Albatross Air Charter Service.
8. Geraldine Page provided the voice for Madame Medusa. Bob Newhart supplied the voice of Bernard and Eva Gabor, who was the voice of Duchess the cat in *The Aristocats,* was Bianca.
9. The helpful little dragonfly is Evinrude.
10. Mr. Snoops is Madame Medusa's bumbling accomplice, voiced by the popular Disney live-action actor Joe Flynn.
11. Madame Medusa's two evil henchmen are crocodiles, Nero and Brutus.
12. The diamond, the world's largest, is referred to as "The Devil's Eye."
13. Medusa hides the jewel in Penny's teddy bear.
14. Penny donates the jewel to a museum.
15. "Someone's Waiting For You."

The Fox and the Hound

July 10, 1981

Questions

1. Who provided the voices of Tod and Copper when they grew up?
2. What is the name of the owl who saved Tod when his mother was killed?
3. To whom does the owl take Tod to be raised properly; and why has the name Tod been chosen for the fox?
4. What creature are Dinky and Boomer trying to catch?
5. What eventually happens to the little creature Dinky and Boomer were trying to catch?
6. What are Dinky and Boomer?
7. Keith Mitchell, who provided the voice of the young Tod, is today acting under what different name?
8. Who is the owner of the dog Copper, and what is the name of the other dog he owns?
9. According to Copper, why can't he and Tod be friends anymore?
10. Why does Tod eventually have to be taken to the game preserve?
11. With whom does Tod fall in love once he is at the game preserve; and who introduces the two to each other?
12. Who comes to the game preserve in order to hunt down Tod?
13. According to Tod, what are the two most beautiful things in the world?
14. At the climax of the movie, Tod saves the day when he fights a what?
15. Tod himself is in danger at the end of the feature. Who saves his life?

The Fox and the Hound

Answers

1. Kurt Russell, the popular Disney teenage actor, was the voice of the hound dog Copper, and Mickey Rooney supplied the voice of Tod the fox.
2. Big Mama is the friendly owl played by Pearl Bailey.
3. Big Mama takes Tod to Widow Tweed. The name Tod is chosen by Widow Tweed because he is just a toddler when he arrives.
4. The little caterpillar, Squeeks.
5. As all good caterpillars do, he changes into a butterfly and flies away.
6. Dinky is a sparrow, and Boomer is a woodpecker.
7. Keith Coogan. He is the grandson of former child star Jackie Coogan.
8. "Fox hater" Amos Slade owns both Copper and Chief.
9. Because he is a hound dog and, according to Copper, he was born to hunt foxes.
10. When Amos Slade and his dog Chief try to capture Tod, Widow Tweed feels he will be safer at the game preserve.
11. The cute little female fox is Vixey, voiced by Sandy Duncan. The two are introduced to each other with the help of Big Mama.
12. Amos Slade and Copper go to the game preserve to try and capture Tod because they blame him for causing an injury to Chief.
13. "Love and friendship."
14. Tod saves Copper from a giant bear.
15. This time Copper saves the day by standing in the path of Amos Slade's rifle.

The Black Cauldron

July 24, 1985

Questions

1. Who are the Cauldron Born?
2. What is Taran's profession, and who does he long to fight?
3. What is the name of the oracular pig, and why is she being chased by the Horned King?
4. The visions brought forth by the pig's magic manifest themselves in what substance?
5. Taran himself looks into a stream of water and an image appears. What does Taran see?
6. What is the name of the Horned King's fawning accomplice?
7. What does Gurgi grab from Taran when they first meet?
8. Where does Taran take the pig to evade the Horned King?
9. What is the name of the beautiful Princess held captive by the Horned King?
10. What is the name of the minstrel that both Taran and the Princess save from the Horned King?
11. Who instructs Taran that the Black Cauldron can be found in the marshes of the Land of Morva?
12. Who were the three witches of Morva?
13. What does Taran trade for possession of the Black Cauldron?
14. According to the witches of Morva, the Black Cauldron can never be destroyed, only the evil powers that possess the Black Cauldron. Who saves the day by destroying its powers?
15. What group reappears at the end of the film and asks for the Black Cauldron back, and what does Taran trade for the return?

The Black Cauldron

Answers

1. The Cauldron Born are an army of once-dead indestructible warriors who come alive through the power of the Black Cauldron.
2. Taran is the assistant pig-keeper for the wizard Dallben, but he longs to fight the evil Horned King.
3. The Horned King wants Hen Wen, the pig, because she knows where to find the Black Cauldron.
4. They appear in water.
5. The image is of Taran, who is represented as a mighty warrior.
6. Creeper.
7. An apple.
8. The Forbidden Forest.
9. The beautiful Eilonwy is prisoner of the Horned King.
10. Flewddur Fflam.
11. The King of the Fair Folk, Eidilleg.
12. Orddu, Orgoch, and Orwen.
13. Taran trades a magic sword that he found while held captive in the Horned King's dungeon. The sword had been attached to the burial chamber of a "fallen king."
14. Gurgi destroyed the Horned King by throwing himself into the Black Cauldron and destroying all of its evil powers.
15. Taran trades the Black Cauldron back to the three witches of Morva in exchange for the revival of Gurgi.

The Great
Mouse Detective

July 2, 1986

Questions

1. Where does *The Great Mouse Detective* take place?
2. What is the name of the hound who helps Basil and Dr. Dawson, and who is his master?
3. Who is the one-legged bat and enforcement officer for Ratigan?
4. Where does Basil live, and where is the evil Ratigan's hideout?
5. Who does Ratigan want to overthrow so that he can become King Ratigan I?
6. What actor provided the voice for Ratigan?
7. Who goes to Basil for help to save her kidnapped father, and what does Ratigan want from this victim?
8. Where does Ratigan send his one-legged accomplice in order to bring back the supplies needed to complete his devilish plot?
9. Where did Dr. Dawson arrive from, and what was he helping celebrate?
10. What is the name of the fat cat Ratigan uses as his executioner?
11. Even though he may actually be this type of creature, what does Ratigan refuse to let others call him?
12. What is the name of the waterfront pub Basil and Dr. Dawson go to in order to track down the one-legged bat?
13. The climactic chase takes place at what famed landmark?
14. As the film concludes, who does Basil ask to be his assistant?
15. What composer provided the music for *The Great Mouse Detective*?

The Great Mouse Detective

Answers

1. London in 1897.
2. Toby is the dog, and his master is the famous Sherlock Holmes who lived upstairs at 221B Baker Street.
3. Fidget.
4. Basil lives in the basement of 221B Baker Street, and Ratigan's hideout is in the city's sewers.
5. Queen Moustoria.
6. Vincent Price.
7. Olivia Flaversham's father, Hiram Flaversham, has been kidnapped by Ratigan because he is a toymaker, and Ratigan wants a robot likeness of the Queen.
8. Ratigan sends Fidget to a toy shop to bring back tools and supplies, so that he can create the robot likeness of Queen Moustoria.
9. Dr. Dawson traveled all the way from India to celebrate Queen Moustoria's fiftieth year of her reign as leader of the Kingdom of Mice.
10. Felicia.
11. Ratigan refuses to have anyone refer to him as a rat.
12. The Rat Trap.
13. In the clock tower of Big Ben.
14. Basil asks Dr. Dawson if he would like to stay on and become his assistant.
15. Henry Mancini.

Oliver & Company

November 18, 1988

Questions

1. Who is the voice of the Artful Dodger who sings "Why Should I Worry"?
2. What crime do Oliver and the Artful Dodger commit in one of the opening scenes, shortly after the two meet?
3. What is the name of the Great Dane, and what actor provides the voice?
4. What is the name of the little Chihuahua?
5. In what city does the film take place?
6. What is Jenny's address?
7. What was the name of Jenny's lavender poodle, and what actress supplied the voice?
8. What was the name of the bulldog?
9. What does the bulldog aspire to be someday?
10. What was the name of the Afghan hound?
11. The dogs' master is Fagin. What was his profession, and where did they live?
12. What was the design of Sykes's car hood ornament?
13. Why was Fagin in trouble with Sykes?
14. Who kidnaps Jenny, and who goes to save the little girl?
15. In the climactic chase scene, what happens to Sykes?

Oliver & Company

1. Billy Joel.
2. The Artful Dodger and Oliver steal some hot dogs from Louie's hot dog cart.
3. Einstein is the Great Dane's name, and Richard Mulligan supplies the voice.
4. Tito.
5. New York City.
6. 1125 Fifth Avenue.
7. Georgette was the pompous lavender poodle voiced by Bette Midler.
8. Francis.
9. Francis aspires to be an actor someday.
10. Rita.
11. Fagin, a scrap dealer by trade, was the dogs' master, and he and the dogs lived at the docks on a barge.
12. Two Great Danes.
13. Fagin borrowed money from Sykes and was given three days to pay it back.
14. Sykes kidnapped Jenny because he knew that her family had plenty of money. However, Fagin and the dogs went and saved Jenny.
15. During the climactic chase scene, Sykes's car crashes off the bridge.

The Little Mermaid

November 17, 1989

1. How many daughters did King Triton have?
2. What is the name of the bumbling seagull, and who provides the voice?
3. What is the name of the little fish that was Ariel's companion during her adventures?
4. According to the seagull, what did he call the fork and pipe Ariel brought to him?
5. What is Sebastian's full name, and what is his official title?
6. What gift does Grimsby present to the Prince aboard the ship?
7. What is the name of Prince Eric's shaggy dog?
8. According to one of the songs, where is it always greener?
9. Ursula, the sea witch, gave Ariel how many days to get the Prince to do what before she could become a human forever?
10. What is the price Ariel has to pay to Ursula for making her human?
11. Where in the castle does Sebastian almost meet his end?
12. What identity did Ursula take to fool the Prince into marrying her?
13. What price did King Triton have to pay for saving his daughter from Ursula?
14. How many Academy Awards did *The Little Mermaid* win, and what is the title of the award-winning song?
15. What early Disney artist received screen credit in *The Little Mermaid* for inspirational sketches he drew fifty years earlier?

The Little Mermaid

Answers

1. Seven: Andrina, Adella, Attina, Alana, Aquata, Arista, and Ariel.
2. Scuttle is the seagull voiced by Buddy Hackett.
3. Flounder.
4. The fork he called a "dinglehopper," and the pipe was a "snarfblatt."
5. Horatio Felonious Crustaceous Ignacious Sebastian, and his title is "court composer."
6. A statue in the Prince's likeness.
7. Max.
8. "The seaweed is always greener in somebody else's lake."
9. Ariel is given human form only until the sun sets on the third day, unless she can get the Prince to kiss her. And "not just any kiss—the kiss of true love."
10. Ursula wants Ariel's golden voice in exchange for giving her legs.
11. The cook in the kitchen, Louie, tries to prepare him for dinner.
12. An Ariel sound-alike named Vanessa, so she could fool the Prince into marrying her.
13. King Triton was willing to give Ursula his trident and crown and the control of his kingdom for the safe release of his daughter.
14. The feature received two Academy Awards: Best Score and Best Song for "Under the Sea."
15. Walt Disney had actually tinkered with the idea of making the Hans Christian Andersen classic *The Little Mermaid* in the 1930s and had Kay Nielsen develop some designs for the character. The artists in the 1980s received inspiration from Nielsen's sketches.

The Rescuers
Down Under
November 10, 1990

Questions

1. What is the name of the giant eagle?
2. What does the giant Eagle give to Cody when he first rescues her?
3. What illegal activity is McLeach engaged in?
4. Bianca and Bernard are from what countries?
5. Who provides the voice of McLeach, and what is the villain's full name?
6. What is the name of McLeach's goanna [lizard] sidekick?
7. Where is the mouse restaurant located?
8. What does Wilbur wear that Orville in the earlier *The Rescuers* doesn't, and vice versa?
9. What relation is Wilbur to Orville?
10. Who provides the voice for Wilbur, and what is Wilbur's company's slogan?
11. Where was the landing spot in Australia to which Wilbur takes Bernard and Bianca?
12. What type of instrument is referred to as the "epidermal tissue disrupter"?
13. What objects belonging to the giant eagle was Wilbur asked to protect?
14. The Australian Jake is what kind of animal?
15. Who wrote the stories on which *The Rescuers* (1977) and *The Rescuers Down Under* (1990) were based?

The Rescuers
Down Under

1. Marahute is the golden eagle that McLeach is after.
2. A golden feather.
3. McLeach has been poaching, taking various wild animals prisoner.
4. Miss Bianca is a delegate from Hungary, and Bernard is from the United States.
5. George C. Scott supplies the voice of Percival C. McLeach.
6. Joanna.
7. The mouse restaurant is located on top of a chandelier in a human restaurant.
8. Wilbur wears a baseball cap and Orville an aviator's cap.
9. They are brothers. The new character was needed because Jim Jordan who had done the voice of Orville in *The Rescuers* (1977) had died.
10. Wilbur is played by John Candy. The airline company has two slogans: "We're Born to Fly" and "A Fair Fare From Here to There."
11. The final landing spot is Mugwomp Flats.
12. A chain saw.
13. Wilbur was asked to protect the golden eagle's eggs, and he did this by sitting on them.
14. A kangaroo mouse.
15. Margery Sharp.

Beauty and the Beast

November 22, 1991

Questions

1. The feature begins when we see a book revealing the name of the story. What was the last Disney animated feature to utilize this technique?
2. Who provided the musical score for the feature?
3. What did the enchantress leave the Beast as his only window to the world?
4. What is the only hope of breaking the spell?
5. What has become of the Beast's servants?
6. What is Belle's favorite pastime?
7. What is the name of Mrs. Potts's son, and what physical feature of his matches that name?
8. Belle offers to exchange herself for what prisoner in the Beast's castle?
9. What is the name of Belle's scatterbrained father whose inventions never seem to work out just right?
10. What is the name of Belle's suitor whose ego is as big as his biceps?
11. According to the song, what does Gaston use in all of his decorating?
12. Who makes Belle feel at home in the castle with the song "Be Our Guest"?
13. According to Gaston, what is Belle's only alternative when it comes to saving her father from being taken to the sanitarium?
14. What character saves Belle and her father from the locked basement of their house after Gaston and the rest of the townspeople have put them there?
15. Who sings the title song, "Beauty and the Beast"?

Beauty and the Beast

Answers

1. *Robin Hood* in 1973.
2. The award-winning team of Howard Ashman and Alan Menken, who provided the music for *The Little Mermaid* (1989). The film captured two Academy Awards: one for Original Score and the other for Best Song, "Beauty and the Beast."
3. He was left with only a mirror as his window to the world.
4. The Beast needs to learn to love someone and for that person to return his love before the last petal on a magic rose falls off. If that last petal does fall off then he will remain a Beast for the rest of his life.
5. The enchantress has turned them all into household objects.
6. She loves to read, and is forever borrowing books from the local book dealer.
7. Chip; because he has a chip on his rim.
8. Her father, who has been imprisoned by the Beast.
9. Maurice.
10. Gaston.
11. Antlers.
12. Lumiere leads the rest of the household objects in a rousing rendition of "Be Our Guest."
13. According to Gaston, the misunderstanding can be cleared up if Belle agrees to marry him.
14. Chip, with the help of Maurice's invention.
15. Angela Lansbury as Mrs. Potts first sings "Beauty and the Beast," and it is sung again under the end titles by Peabo Bryson and Celine Dion.

Aladdin

November 1992

Questions

1. What kind of animal does Aladdin have as a pet?
2. How does the evil Jafar get the Sultan to do his bidding?
3. Jafar sends Aladdin into the Cave of Wonders to get what?
4. What is Aladdin's first wish of the genie?
5. What does Jasmine take in the marketplace, causing Aladdin to have to come to her rescue?

Aladdin

· · · · · · · · · · · · ·

Answers

1. His pet is Abu, a monkey.
2. He hypnotizes the Sultan with his cobra-headed staff.
3. A lamp.
4. He wishes to be a prince so he can marry the Princess Jasmine.
5. An apple.

Treasure Island

July 19, 1950

Questions

1. Who played the roles of Jim Hawkins and Long John Silver?
2. Whose treasure is everyone searching for, and who has secretly recovered the bounty years before?
3. What are the names of the ship's captain and the doctor?
4. Where did Jim Hawkins work when he received the treasure map?
5. What is the name of the ship?

Treasure Island

Answers

1. Bobby Driscoll played Jim Hawkins, and Robert Newton was pirate Long John Silver.
2. Ben Gunn actually discovered Captain Flint's treasure. He had been marooned on the island some years previously by Long John Silver.
3. They are Captain Smollett and Doctor Livesey.
4. At the Admiral Benbow Inn, where he was given the map by Captain Billy Bones.
5. The *Hispaniola*.

20,000 Leagues Under the Sea

··

December 23, 1954

Questions

1. Who played the part of Ned Land, and what was the name of his adopted seal?
2. What were the names of Captain Nemo's submarine and his South Sea hideaway, and who portrayed the cunning captain?
3. What is the name of the frigate that Ned Land, Professor Aronnax, and Conseil are on before they are captured by Captain Nemo?
4. The son of one of Walt Disney's earliest competitors directed *20,000 Leagues Under the Sea.* Can you name him?
5. How many Academy Awards did *20,000 Leagues Under the Sea* win?

20,000 Leagues Under the Sea

Answers

1. Kirk Douglas played the harpooner Ned Land, and his adopted seal was named Esmeralda.
2. The submarine was the *Nautilus,* and the South Sea hideaway was Vulcania. James Mason portrayed the captain and designer of the ship.
3. The *Abraham Lincoln.*
4. Richard Fleischer directed the film. His father, Max Fleischer, was the animator whose *Out of the Inkwell* series inspired Walt Disney to develop his *Alice Comedy* series.
5. The picture won two Academy Awards, one for Best Special Effects and one for Best Set/Art Direction.

Davy Crockett, King of the Wild Frontier

May 25, 1955

Questions

1. What was the hit title song for the movie *Davy Crockett, King of the Wild Frontier*?
2. What type of hat became popular because of the movie?
3. Who asked Davy Crockett to help fight the Indians?
4. Who does Davy Crockett help at the Alamo?
5. What were the individual titles of the three Disney television shows that were strung together to make *Davy Crockett, King of the Wild Frontier*?

Davy Crockett, King of the Wild Frontier

Answers

1. "The Ballad of Davy Crockett," written by George Bruns and Tom Blackburn.
2. The coonskin cap.
3. General Andrew Jackson asked Davy to fight Chief Red Stick. But Davy Crockett did one better; instead of going to war with the Indians, he convinced them to sign a peace treaty.
4. Colonel Jim Bowie.
5. *Davy Crockett Indian Fighter, Davy Crockett Goes to Congress,* and *Davy Crockett at the Alamo.*

Old Yeller

December 25, 1957

Questions

1. In what state was the movie set?
2. Who played the role of Travis and Arliss Coates's father, and why was he gone for a good portion of the film?
3. What popular regulars from Mickey Mouse Club serials played the parts of Arliss and Travis Coates?
4. Who was asked by the men in the town to watch out for the women and children while the men were gone?
5. Why was Old Yeller put to rest by one of the Coates boys?

Old Yeller

Answers

1. Texas in 1869.
2. Fess Parker played the role of Jim Coates, and he was on a cattle drive for a good portion of the movie.
3. Kevin Corcoran played the role of Arliss Coates, and Tommy Kirk played Travis.
4. Bud Searcy, who was basically no help at all.
5. Old Yeller contracted rabies and was eventually shot by Travis Coates.

The Shaggy Dog

March 19, 1959

Questions

1. What actor makes his Disney debut as Wilson Daniels, and what is Daniels's profession?
2. What is the name of the next door neighbor Franceska Andrassy's shaggy dog?
3. What device transforms Wilby Daniels into the Shaggy Dog?
4. What is the Latin inscription that effects the transformation?
5. What Mouseketeer made her Disney feature-film debut in the role of Allison D'Alessio?

The Shaggy Dog

Answers

1. Fred MacMurray plays Wilson Daniels, a postman, but we never see him working.
2. Chiffon is the dog next door.
3. A legendary and bewitched ring, once owned by the Borgia family.
4. "In canis corpore transmuto."
5. America's sweetheart, Annette Funicello.

Swiss Family Robinson

December 21, 1960

Questions

1. Who was the author of the book *The Swiss Family Robinson?*
2. Can you name the actors who portrayed the three Robinson boys and their father, and the actress who played the mother?
3. What was the family's destination before the storm forced them to the tropical island?
4. What was the name of the young girl two of the Robinson boys rescue from a band of pirates?
5. Who was the only Robinson to leave the island?

Swiss Family Robinson

Answers

1. Johann Wyss.
2. Fritz was played by James MacArthur; Ernst was played by Tommy Kirk; Kevin Corcoran played Francis. The father was portrayed by John Mills, and Dorothy Maguire played the mother.
3. The family was going to settle in New Guinea.
4. Roberta, played by Janet Munro, was saved by Fritz and Ernst.
5. The entire family had the opportunity to leave, but only Ernst left so he could attend university.

The Absent-Minded Professor

March 16, 1961

Questions

1. What event does the professor miss while working on his experiments in his lab?
2. What actor portrays the absent-minded professor, and what is the character's name?
3. What type of car does the professor drive?
4. What revolutionary new product does the professor invent?
5. Who play the roles of Alonzo Hawk and his son Biff?

The Absent-Minded Professor

Answers

1. The professor misses his wedding.
2. Fred MacMurray is Professor Ned Brainard.
3. The professor was famous for his Model T Ford.
4. "Flubber," short for flying rubber.
5. Keenan Wynn plays the unscrupulous Alonzo Hawk, and Disney regular Tommy Kirk is his son Biff Hawk.

The Parent Trap

June 21, 1961

Questions

1. What actress plays the dual role of Sharon McKendrick and Susan Evers?
2. Which one of the girls lives with her mother and which one lives with her father, and where do they live?
3. Where do the girls meet?
4. What is the title of the song the sisters sing in an effort to bring their parents back together again?
5. What are the girls doing in the final scene?

The Parent Trap

Answers

1. Hayley Mills.
2. Sharon McKendrick lives with her mother in Boston, and Susan Evers lives with her father in California.
3. At Camp Inch summer camp.
4. "Let's Get Together."
5. Serving as bridesmaids at their parents' wedding.

Mary Poppins

August 27, 1964

Questions

1. What actress played the famous nanny who was "practically perfect in every way"?
2. What are the names of the two Banks children?
3. What is the name of the friendly chimney sweep, and what is he doing at the beginning of the film?
4. Where does George Banks work, and what is his wife's name?
5. What is so unusual about Mary Poppins's umbrella handle?
6. Who joins Dick Van Dyke in his "Jolly Holiday" dance?
7. According to the song, what "helps the medicine go down"?
8. What does the old bird woman charge for her birdseed?
9. Where does the bird woman sell her wares?
10. What is the title of the Academy Award—winning song from the production?

Mary Poppins

Answers

1. Julie Andrews, who won a Best Actress Academy Award for her portrayal.
2. Jane and Michael.
3. Bert, the chimney sweep, played by Dick Van Dyke, is playing a one-man band.
4. He works at the Dawes, Tomes, Mousely, Grubbs Fidelity Fiduciary Bank, and his wife is named Winifred.
5. It is a parrot head, and it talks!
6. The penguin waiters at the outdoor cafe.
7. "A Spoonful of Sugar."
8. Tuppence a bag.
9. On the steps of St. Paul's Cathedral in London.
10. "Chim Chim Cher-ee," written by the Sherman Brothers.

The Happiest Millionaire

June 23, 1967

Questions

1. In what city and when does the movie take place?
2. What is the name of the butler who steals the show, and what actor plays the role?
3. What popular Disney actor portrays the part of Anthony J. Drexel Biddle?
4. How many children do the Biddles have, and how many alligators does Anthony J. Drexel Biddle own?
5. What is imprinted on the Biddles' sweatshirts?

The Happiest Millionaire

Answers

1. Philadelphia in 1917.
2. Tommy Steele portrays the very entertaining butler, John Lawless, who came straight off the boat from Ireland.
3. Fred MacMurray plays the eccentric millionaire.
4. The Biddles have three children: Cordelia, Tony, and Livingston. Anthony J. Drexel Biddle also has twelve alligators from Florida; his favorite is named George.
5. "Biddle Bible Class."

The Love Bug

March 13, 1969

Questions

1. What number was on the little Volkswagen, and who chose it?
2. What is the name of the famous Volkswagen?
3. What actor played the role of Tennessee Steinmetz, and who portrayed the scoundrel Thorndyke?
4. Who is the race car driver owner of The Love Bug?
5. The Love Bug became somewhat of a regular star for Disney fans; in fact, three theatrical sequels were made. Can you name them?

The Love Bug

Answers

1. The number was "53," and it was given to the car by the auto mechanic Tennessee Steinmetz.
2. Herbie.
3. Buddy Hackett played Tennessee Steinmetz, and David Tomlinson, also known for his portrayal of Mr. Banks in *Mary Poppins* in 1964, was the scheming Thorndyke.
4. Race car driver Jim Douglas was played by Dean Jones.
5. *Herbie Rides Again* (1974); *Herbie Goes to Monte Carlo* (1977); and *Herbie Goes Bananas* (1980).

Candleshoe

February 10, 1978

Questions

1. What actress played the troublesome Casey Brown, who also passed herself off as Lady Margaret?
2. What legendary actress played the role of Lady St. Edmund?
3. Who was Lady St. Edmund's all-purpose butler, gardener, and chauffeur?
4. Whose treasure were they all searching for?
5. What is the name of the villain who tried to convince Lady St. Edmund that Casey Brown was actually her long-lost granddaughter, Lady Margaret?

Candleshoe

Answers

1. Jodie Foster played the double role of Casey Brown, street kid, and the refined Lady Margaret.
2. Helen Hayes.
3. David Niven played the role of Priory.
4. The treasure of Captain Joshua St. Edmund.
5. Bundage.

The Black Hole

December 21, 1979

Questions

1. *The Black Hole* was the first Disney film to get what rating?
2. What is the name of the evil captain, and what is the name of his ship?
3. What is the name of the spacecraft that discovers the lost ship, and who is its captain?
4. What is the name of the doctor, and how was he disposed of?
5. What is the name of the hovering "good guy" robot aboard the ship, who was voiced by Roddy McDowall?

The Black Hole

Answers

1. A PG rating.
2. Captain Reinhardt is played by Maximilian Schell, and his ship is the *Cygnus*.
3. The spacecraft is the *Palomino*, and its captain is named Holland, played by Robert Forster.
4. Doctor Durant, played by Anthony Perkins, was disposed of by Captain Reinhardt's henchman, a hovering robot named Maximillian.
5. The hovering robot was V.I.N.Cent.

Who Framed Roger Rabbit

June 22, 1988

Questions

1. Who is Roger accused of killing?
2. For what cartoon studio does Roger work?
3. What is the name of the place where all the Toons live?
4. What is the name of the detective who is hired to follow Roger's wife, Jessica?
5. What is the name of the liquid that Toons dread?

Who Framed Roger Rabbit

Answers

1. Marvin Acme.
2. Maroon Studios.
3. Toontown.
4. Eddie Valiant.
5. Dip!

Dick Tracy

June 15, 1990

Questions

1. What actor brought Chester Gould's famous comic strip detective, Dick Tracy, to life?
2. What crime baron wants Tracy out of the way?
3. What name does the Kid finally select?
4. Which singer/actress played the role of Breathless Mahoney?
5. The song title "Sooner or Later" had been used earlier (for a different song) in what Disney film?

Dick Tracy

1. Warren Beatty.
2. Big Boy Caprice, played by Al Pacino.
3. Dick Tracy, Jr.
4. Madonna.
5. *Song of the South* (1946).

The Rocketeer

June 21, 1991

Questions

1. Who plays the role of Cliff Secord, also known as the Rocketeer?
2. What was Cliff Secord's profession before he became a great hero?
3. Who plays the part of Neville Sinclair?
4. Who is the gangster that Neville Sinclair hires to get the rocket pack back?
5. Where does Neville Sinclair take Cliff Secord's girlfriend, Jenny, to get information on the rocket pack?

The Rocketeer

Answers

1. Bill Campbell plays the role of Cliff Secord.
2. Cliff Secord was a barnstorming pilot at the Bigelow Air Circus in Los Angeles, California, prior to becoming the Rocketeer.
3. Timothy Dalton.
4. Eddie Valentine.
5. The South Seas Club.

Disney on Television

Questions

1. What was the name of the first program Walt Disney ever made for television, and when was it shown?
2. What was the title of the first weekly Walt Disney series?
3. On what network and on what evening did the series run?
4. Who was the original host of the Disney television series?
5. What brand of peanut butter was a sponsor for that series?
6. When did the title of the series first change?
7. In what year did the original Mickey Mouse Club premiere?
8. How many years did the original Mickey Mouse Club air?
9. New versions of the Mickey Mouse Club aired first in what years?
10. You know them as Jimmie, Roy, Darlene, Cubby, Annette, Tommy, Sharon, Doreen, Lonnie, Bobby, and Karen. What were their last names?
11. Who wrote the Mickey Mouse Club's theme song?
12. On the original Mickey Mouse Club series, each day had a different theme. Can you name them?
13. What Disney character used to strike the gong each day to open the original Mickey Mouse Club?
14. A popular miniseries on the Mickey Mouse Club was *The Adventures of Spin and Marty*. What two stars played the roles?
15. Do you know the last names of Spin and Marty?
16. What was the name of the ranch where *The Adventures of Spin and Marty* was set?
17. After the series had been established as a hit, a new character was added, named "Moochie." Who played this role?
18. Another popular miniseries was *The Hardy Boys*. What two stars played the roles of Frank and Joe?
19. Who were the two hosts of the Mickey Mouse Club?
20. Who taught us how to spell "encyclopedia" on the Mickey Mouse Club?
21. For what show did Walt Disney win his first Emmy Award for Best Program of the Year?
22. What network televised the grand opening ceremonies from Disneyland on July 17, 1955?

23. What future American president was one of the hosts of the opening of Disneyland TV special?

24. When did the incredibly popular Davy Crockett make his television debut?

25. What actor played Davy Crockett?

26. What was the name of Davy Crockett's trustworthy sidekick, and what actor portrayed him?

27. What did Davy Crockett call his rifle?

28. What most people don't realize is that Walt Disney made only three Davy Crockett episodes that first season. Davy was brought back the next year in two more episodes. In one of those episodes he's in a keelboat race; what is the name of the character he races?

29. Davy Crockett's keelboat race was held on what river?

30. Another series from the fifties was *Zorro*. What year did our masked hero make his debut?

31. What was Zorro's other name, and what actor played the part?

32. What was the name of the Commandante who was Zorro's foe?

33. What was the name of this evil Commandante's sidekick, and what was the name of Zorro's sidekick?

34. What were the names of Zorro's two horses?

35. "Fresh-Up Freddie" was an animated character designed by the Disney staff for which *Zorro* sponsor?

36. What letter would Zorro slash with his sword?

37. What actor, and later author, played the role of Texas John Slaughter, fearless lawman, on a Disney miniseries?

38. Leslie Nielsen portrayed what legendary Revolutionary War patriot on a Disney miniseries?

39. The 1960–61 season's most popular miniseries was *Daniel Boone*. Who played the role of this famous pioneer?

40. Another popular miniseries was *The Nine Lives of Elfego Baca*. What actor portrayed the role?

41. In 1961 the weekly series made its first network change. To what network did the weekly show move, and what was the new title?

42. What animated character made his debut on the very first episode of the 1961–62 season?

43. What was the Scarecrow of Romney Marsh's real name, and who portrayed the role?

44. A successful miniseries of 1964–65 was *Gallagher*. Who played the part of this budding newspaperman of the early 1900s?

45. Who played the part of the helicopter traffic reporter in the 1969 show *My Dog, The Thief?*

46. Do you remember the name of the dog from *My Dog, the Thief?*

47. Disney animator Ward Kimball produced and directed what syndicated cartoon series in the 1970s?

48. When did The Disney Channel make its debut, and for how many hours a day was it on?

49. What is the name of the exercise show on The Disney Channel?

50. In 1985 Touchstone, the new Disney production arm, ventured into prime-time programming. What was their first weekly comedy show?

51. When the *Magical World of Disney* aired as a series in the 1980s, who was the host?

52. In 1985 Disney returned to children's programming with what two cartoon shows?

53. In what city does *The Golden Girls* take place?

54. What is the hometown of Rose Nyland, one of the lovable stars of *The Golden Girls?*

55. What is the name of the dog on *Empty Nest?*

56. What popular singing group was created from members of The Disney Channel's Mickey Mouse Club?

57. *Avonlea,* on The Disney Channel, is a sequel to what mini-series starring Megan Follows?

58. The popular Disney Channel show *Avonlea* is set in what Canadian province?

59. What was the title of the short-lived program featuring a zany hotel and its guests?

60. What new duck character headed a cartoon series beginning in 1991?

Disney on Television

1. *One Hour in Wonderland* on December 25, 1950.
2. *Disneyland* premiered October 27, 1954.
3. *Disneyland* was on ABC on Wednesdays.
4. Walt Disney himself handled the hosting chores from the first show in 1954 until his death in 1966.
5. Peter Pan Peanut Butter.
6. During the 1959–1960 season it was renamed *Walt Disney Presents*.
7. The popular *Mickey Mouse Club* show premiered on October 3, 1955.
8. For four years, from 1955 through 1959.
9. The show made a comeback in 1977 and again in 1989, with whole new casts of Mouseketeers.
10. The stars of the Club were Jimmie Dodd, Roy Williams, Darlene Gillespie, Carl "Cubby" O'Brien, Annette Funicello, Tommy Cole, Sharon Baird, Doreen Tracey, Lonnie Burr, Bobby Burgess, and Karen Pendleton.
11. "The Mickey Mouse Club March" was written by Jimmie Dodd.
12. Monday was "Fun with Music Day"; Tuesday was "Guest Star Day"; Wednesday was "Anything Can Happen Day"; Thursday was "Circus Day"; and Friday was "Talent Roundup Day."
13. Donald Duck. There were many versions of the segment, and the audience never knew quite what to expect when Donald struck the gong.
14. Tim Considine played Spin, and David Stollery Marty.
15. Spin Evans and Marty Markham.
16. Triple R Ranch.
17. Kevin Corcoran.
18. Frank and Joe Hardy were played by Tim Considine and Tommy Kirk.
19. Roy Williams, a Disney artist and story man, was the "Big Mooseketeer," and Jimmie Dodd was the "Head Mouseketeer."
20. Jiminy Cricket.
21. Walt Disney received his first Emmy Award for the December

8, 1954, *Operation Undersea,* a show on the making of *20,000 Leagues Under the Sea* (1954).

22. ABC aired *Dateline Disneyland* on July 17, 1955.
23. Ronald Reagan, then a Hollywood actor, performed emcee chores, along with Art Linkletter and Bob Cummings.
24. The Davy Crockett miniseries premiered on December 15, 1954.
25. Fess Parker.
26. George Russel, played by Buddy Ebsen. Buddy Ebsen and James Arness were originally up for the role of Davy Crockett, but Walt Disney chose Fess Parker.
27. "Old Betsy."
28. In "Davy Crockett's Keelboat Race" on November 16, 1955, Davy went up against the King of the River, Mike Fink, played by Jeff York.
29. The Mississippi River.
30. 1957.
31. Guy Williams played the role of Zorro, who was also known as Don Diego de la Vega.
32. The evil Commandante Monastario, played by Britt Lomond.
33. The evil Commandante's sidekick was Sergeant Garcia, and Zorro's sidekick was Bernardo.
34. Tornado and Phantom; one black and the other white.
35. Seven-Up.
36. "Z."
37. Texas John Slaughter was played by Tom Tryon.
38. "The Swamp Fox" (General Francis Marion).
39. Dewey Martin.
40. Robert Loggia.
41. The series moved to NBC, where it remained for the next twenty years, and the new title was *Walt Disney's Wonderful World of Color.*
42. Ludwig Von Drake.
43. Dr. Christopher Syn, played by Patrick McGoohan.
44. Roger Mobley.
45. Dwayne Hickman.
46. The St. Bernard, Barabbas.
47. *The Mouse Factory.*
48. The Disney Channel first aired on April 18, 1983, for sixteen hours a day.
49. *Mousercise.*
50. *The Golden Girls.*
51. Michael Eisner, chairman of The Walt Disney Company.

52. *The Wuzzles* and *Disney's Adventures of the Gummi Bears.*
53. Miami, Florida.
54. St. Olaf, Minnesota.
55. Dreyfuss, who was named in 1991 as the "National Spokes-Dog" for the American Humane Society.
56. The Party.
57. *Anne of Green Gables* and *Anne of Avonlea.*
58. Prince Edward Island.
59. *The Nutt House.*
60. Darkwing Duck.

Main Street, USA

Questions

1. Name one of the four railroad engines that make up the Disneyland Railroad.
2. Where was Walt Disney's apartment on Main Street, USA?
3. What was the cost of building Disneyland, and how long did it take to build?
4. Who sponsored the Great Moments with Mr. Lincoln attraction at the 1964–65 New York World's Fair, and where was it situated when it was moved to Disneyland?
5. How many attractions were open for the grand opening of Disneyland?

Answers

1. The four engines are the "C. K. Holliday," the "E. P. Ripley," the "Ernest S. Marsh," and the "Fred Gurley," names of founders and executives of the Santa Fe Railroad.
2. Above the Fire House, next to Town Square.
3. The cost was $17 million. The construction took a year, with the opening day being July 17, 1955.
4. The state of Illinois; once the attraction arrived at Disneyland guests could enjoy it at the Main Street Opera House.
5. When Disneyland opened its doors there were eighteen paid and three free attractions.

Fantasyland

Questions

1. What is the name of the carrousel in the middle of Fantasyland's court?
2. What famous composers wrote the music for the It's a Small World attraction?
3. What Fantasyland attraction did President Harry Truman refuse to ride during his visit to Disneyland?
4. In what year did the first thrill attraction at Disneyland, the Matterhorn, open?
5. What is the name of the turreted castle that serves as the entrance to Fantasyland?

Fantasyland

·······················

Answers

1. King Arthur Carrousel.
2. The Sherman Brothers (whose music was also featured in *Mary Poppins* in 1964).
3. Dumbo the Flying Elephant, because the elephant symbolized the Republican Party.
4. 1959.
5. Sleeping Beauty Castle, though in one of his early TV shows showing construction progress of Disneyland, Walt Disney called it Snow White's Castle.

Adventureland

· ·

Questions

1. What Hollywood movie inspired the development of the Jungle Cruise?
2. What Adventureland attraction has the inhabitants looking for a hand-out?
3. When did the Swiss Family Treehouse make its debut, and what star of the Disney film was on hand to make the official dedication?
4. Adventureland was inspired by what Disney live-action film series?
5. The Enchanted Tiki Room was heralded as being the first to feature what Disney-invented process for controlling the movements of the birds, flowers, and tiki gods?

Adventureland

· ·

Answers

1. *The African Queen,* starring Humphrey Bogart and Katharine Hepburn.
2. The Jungle Cruise with its ever-hungry crocodiles.
3. John Mills, star of the *Swiss Family Robinson* movie of 1960, was on hand in 1962 for the ceremony.
4. *True-Life Adventures.*
5. *Audio-Animatronics,* a process later refined and used with even greater sophistication (Abraham Lincoln, Pirates of the Caribbean, Country Bear Jamboree, Splash Mountain, etc.).

Frontierland

·························

Questions

1. What is the name of the riverboat that sails the Rivers of America, and on opening day who did the honors of breaking the ceremonial bottle over the riverboat's stern?
2. What Frontierland attraction is featured in the *Guinness Book of World Records* for the largest number of performances for a theatrical show?
3. The Davy Crockett series helped inspire what attractions?
4. The Big Thunder Mountain Railroad runaway train occupies the site of what previous attraction?
5. Who was the original comedian in the Golden Horseshoe Revue? His name can also be found on one of the second-story windows on Main Street, USA.

Frontierland

Answers

1. The *Mark Twain*. Actress Irene Dunne helped christen the *Mark Twain* on July 17, 1955. The "unofficial maiden voyage" took place on July 13, 1955, four days prior to the grand opening of Disneyland, for Walt and Lillian Disney's thirtieth wedding anniversary.
2. The Golden Horseshoe Revue from 1955 through 1986, with some 50,000 performances.
3. The Mike Fink Keelboats and Davy Crockett's Explorer Canoes.
4. The Rainbow Cavern's Mine Train used to occupy the Big Thunder Mountain Railroad site.
5. Wally Boag, who also provided the voice for one of the host parrots in the Enchanted Tiki Room.

Tomorrowland

·······································

Questions

1. What company sponsored the Progressland Show at the 1964–65 New York World's Fair, and what was the show named once it reached Disneyland?
2. When did the popular Monorail make its "maiden voyage"?
3. In a Circle-Vision film, how many screens are utilized for the 360-degree film?
4. What popular Tomorrowland attraction opened January 12, 1987?
5. What is the 3-D adventure-thriller starring Michael Jackson, and where is it shown?

Tomorrowland

······························

Answers

1. General Electric sponsored the show, and it was known as the Carousel of Progress.

2. On June 14, 1959; it was referred to as Disney's "Highway in the Sky."

3. Nine. In the 1950s, when the process was called Circarama, eleven screens were needed, but refinements of the process cut it down to nine.

4. The Star Tours attraction, and to celebrate Disneyland put together a sixty-hour-long party.

5. The 3-D adventure *Captain EO* can be seen at the Magic Eye Theatre.

New Orleans Square

Questions

1. On what New Orleans Square attraction do you travel up a waterfall?
2. What is the theme song of Pirates of the Caribbean?
3. Guests are transported through The Haunted Mansion in vehicles known as what?
4. From what restaurant can guests view part of Pirates of the Caribbean?
5. The mayor of what city traveled to Disneyland to help Walt Disney dedicate New Orleans Square?

New Orleans Square

···

Answers

1. Pirates of the Caribbean.
2. "Yo Ho, Yo Ho, A Pirate's Life for Me."
3. The Haunted Mansion's vehicles are known as "Doom Buggies."
4. The Blue Bayou.
5. You should be able to guess this one—New Orleans.

Critter Country

Questions

1. What is the name given to the top of Splash Mountain?
2. What character is bothered by bees in Splash Mountain?
3. What is the name of the snoring bear in Disneyland's Splash Mountain?
4. What is the name of the opening act of the Country Bear Jamboree?
5. Splash Mountain is based on what classic Disney film?

© Walt Disney Productions

Critter Country

· ·

Answers

1. Chickapin Hill.
2. Brer Bear.
3. Rufus; his cave had been on the site prior to the building of Splash Mountain.
4. "The Five Bear Rugs," starring Zeke, Zeb, Fred, Ted, and Tennessee.
5. *Song of the South* (1946).

Main Street, USA

Questions

1. Can you name one of the four railroad engines that circle the park?
2. What small Missouri town gave Walt Disney the original inspiration for Main Street, USA?
3. Name the four types of vehicles available for guests riding up Main Street.
4. What Main Street attraction provides visitors with a look at Walt Disney's life and career?
5. Who gave the dedication speech at the opening of Walt Disney World?

Main Street, USA

Answers

1. The *Walter E. Disney,* the *Lilly Belle,* the *Roy O. Disney,* and the *Roger E. Broggie.* Broggie was the technician who ran the machine shop at the Disney Studio and who helped Walt with his train hobby.

2. Marceline, Missouri, a town the Disney family moved to when he was only four.

3. The horseless carriages, horse-drawn streetcars, double-decker bus and a fire engine.

4. The Walt Disney Story, which opened in 1973, provides guests with a glance at the man behind the Mouse, Walter Elias Disney.

5. Roy O. Disney, Walt's brother and long-time business partner.

Fantasyland

Questions

1. What restaurant can be found on the second floor of Cinderella Castle, and what film inspired it?
2. What attraction takes visitors on a whimsical journey through Never Land?
3. What is considered the "wildest" ride in all of Fantasyland?
4. In the 20,000 Leagues Under the Sea attraction, who is your legendary captain and where does he take his guests?
5. What Fantasyland attraction made its debut at Walt Disney World and then was sent to Tokyo Disneyland?

Fantasyland

* * *

Answers

1. King Stefan's Banquet Hall from the 1959 feature *Sleeping Beauty.*
2. Peter Pan's Flight takes you above the streets of London and then past "the second star to the right and straight on 'til morning."
3. Mr. Toad's Wild Ride.
4. Captain Nemo attempts to take guests to his South Seas hideaway, Vulcania.
5. The Mickey Mouse Revue was moved to Tokyo Disneyland.

Adventureland

· ·

Questions

1. What Adventureland attraction was added two years after the park's opening because of its popularity at Disneyland?
2. What is the name of the waterfall in The Jungle Cruise?
3. What country's flag flies on top of the Swiss Family Tree-house?
4. Caribbean Plaza, an area of Adventureland, is home to what popular attraction?
5. According to the guides on the Jungle Cruise, what is the name of the headhunter who is "willing to trade three of his heads for one of yours"?

Adventureland

· ·

Answers

1. Pirates of the Caribbean did not open until December 15, 1973.
2. Schweitzer Falls.
3. A Swiss flag.
4. Pirates of the Caribbean.
5. The headhunter known as Chief Namee. (He used to be known as Joe or Sam.)

Frontierland

....

Questions

1. What Frontierland attraction had its premiere first at Walt Disney World and then in Disneyland the following year?
2. Where do the Country Bear Jamboree singers perform, and who is your host?
3. What is the highest "mountain" in all of Florida?
4. What are the names of the fort and the working mill located on Tom Sawyer Island?
5. How many different types of water craft travel the Rivers of America?

Frontierland

· ·

Answers

1. The Country Bear Jamboree.
2. Grizzly Hall is the home of the Country Bear Jamboree performers, and your host is Henry.
3. Big Thunder Mountain, home of Big Thunder Mountain Railroad.
4. The fort is Fort Sam Clemens, and the mill is Harper's Mill.
5. The Richard F. Irvine riverboat, the Mike Fink Keel Boats, Tom Sawyer Island Rafts, and Davy Crockett's Explorer Canoes.

Liberty Square

Questions

1. What is the name of the riverboat that sails the Rivers of America?
2. How many "Happy Haunts" can be found inside The Haunted Mansion?
3. What is the name of the large oak tree that stands in the courtyard of Liberty Square? It is named after a tree in what Disney film?
4. The Hall of Presidents recreates the look of what two colonial cities, and what date is on top of the Hall of Presidents building?
5. Since the opening of Walt Disney World how many new presidents have been added to The Hall of Presidents?

Liberty Square

Answers

1. The *Richard F. Irvine*. At one time there were two stern-wheelers, the other being the *Admiral Joe Fowler*.
2. According to the story, The Haunted Mansion is home to "999 Happy Haunts"; but the story goes on to say that there is always room for one more!
3. The tree is known as The Liberty Tree, after the one in *Johnny Tremain* (1957).
4. Philadelphia and Boston, and the date is 1787, the year the Constitution of the United States was framed.
5. To date four Presidents: Gerald Ford, Jimmy Carter, Ronald Reagan, and George Bush.

Tomorrowland

Questions

1. If you board the Skyway in Tomorrowland, where does it take you?
2. Which Tomorrowland attraction was moved from Disneyland to the Walt Disney World Magic Kingdom?
3. What attraction takes you through the history of aviation, and who sponsors it?
4. What attraction is atop the WEDWay PeopleMover?
5. The attraction known as Autopia at Disneyland has what different name at the Walt Disney World Magic Kingdom?

Tomorrowland

· ·

Answers

1. You will end up in Fantasyland.
2. The Carousel of Progress debuted first at the New York World's Fair (1964–65) and then was moved to Disneyland, and in 1975 to the Walt Disney World Magic Kingdom.
3. Delta Airlines sponsors Dreamflight.
4. Star Jets.
5. Grand Prix Raceway.

Mickey's Starland

Questions

1. What was Mickey's Starland originally called when it opened in 1988?
2. The site of Mickey's Starland is Duckburg, USA. What is the town's motto?
3. Who was the founder of Duckburg, USA?
4. Where can guests greet Mickey live and in person in Mickey's Starland?
5. According to the sign, what is the population of Duckburg, USA?

Mickey's Starland

Answers

1. Mickey's Birthdayland, in honor of the famous Mouse's six-tieth birthday.
2. The motto of Duckburg, USA is "A town that's everything it's quacked up to be."
3. Cornelius Coot. There is a statue of him in the town square.
4. In his dressing room at Mickey's Hollywood Theatre.
5. The population of Duckburg, USA is "Bill'ions and still growing."

Walt Disney World EPCOT Center
Future World

Questions

1. Who sponsors Spaceship Earth?
2. What science-fiction author helped write the concept for Spaceship Earth?
3. What is the name of the friendly robot in CommuniCore East?
4. What decade-long poll originated at the Electronic Forum in CommuniCore?
5. What provides 15 percent of the energy needed to run the ride vehicles in Universe of Energy?
6. Wonders of Life, the newest pavilion in Future World, is located between what other pavilions?
7. When you visit Horizons, you are given the chance to vote on visiting what three twenty-first century living environments?
8. What is the attraction, using flight simulator technology, in Wonders of Life that takes guests on an action-packed journey through the human body?
9. What attraction in Wonders of Life delves into the operation of the brain of a twelve-year old boy?
10. Who narrates the Wonders of Life film *The Making of Me*?
11. What company sponsors the World of Motion?
12. What was the name of the original 3-D movie shown at Journey into Imagination?
13. Who are your hosts for Journey into Imagination?
14. What year did *Captain EO* premiere, and who directed and produced it?
15. Michael Jackson, who plays Captain EO, wrote two songs for the 3-D spectacular. Can you name one of them?
16. What is the name of the boat tour within The Land?
17. Who is your hostess at The Kitchen Kabaret?
18. What is the name of the movie featured at the Harvest Theater in The Land?
19. What company sponsors The Living Seas, and what is the name of the oceanic research base?
20. What is the name of the restaurant in The Living Seas?

Future World

Answers

1. AT&T.
2. Ray Bradbury.
3. The friendly robot is SMRT-1.
4. The Person of the Century.
5. Photovoltaic or solar cells on the top of the building.
6. Wonders of Life is situated between Universe of Energy and Horizons.
7. The three are: space (Brava Centauri), desert (Mesa Verde), and ocean (Sea Castle).
8. Body Wars.
9. Cranium Command.
10. The narrator is Martin Short.
11. General Motors.
12. *Magic Journeys;* it is currently being shown in Fantasyland at the Walt Disney World Magic Kingdom.
13. Figment and Dreamfinder.
14. 1986; directed by Francis Ford Coppola and produced by George Lucas.
15. "We Are Here to Change the World" and "Another Part of Me."
16. Listen to the Land.
17. Bonnie Appetit is your hostess.
18. *Symbiosis.*
19. United Technologies, and the ocean research center is Sea Base Alpha.
20. The Coral Reef Restaurant.

World Showcase

·······································

Questions

1. Which two countries are at the gateways of World Showcase?
2. How many countries in all are represented in World Showcase?
3. In the American Adventure, what figure appears to walk (a first for Disney's *Audio-Animatronics*)?
4. Who are the hosts for the American Adventure?
5. What is the boat ride guests can take in Mexico?
6. What is the name of the restaurant located inside Mexico?
7. What is the name of the high seas adventure ride at Norway?
8. What is the name of the popular restaurant at Italy, and what is the statue outside the restaurant?
9. What Italian city was the inspiration for the pavilion, and what is the name of the famous palace?
10. What is the name of the 360-degree movie at China?
11. The Ceremonial Gate at Japan is a replica of what historical shrine?
12. In what country's restaurant is your food prepared right at your table?
13. Which is the only country in World Showcase whose pavilion has governmental rather than private sponsorship?
14. What French city gave Disney the inspiration for that country's pavilion?
15. What is the name of the movie guests can view in France?
16. What is the name of the popular pub at the United Kingdom?
17. What is the name of the Circle-Vision 360-degree movie at Canada?
18. In what country would you find a replica of the Château Laurier?
19. Between what two countries do guests have to pass in order to get to the Yacht and Beach Club Resorts?
20. The Laserphonic Fantasy show was replaced by what night-time show around World Showcase Lagoon?

World Showcase

Answers

1. Mexico and Canada.
2. Eleven: Mexico, Norway, China, Germany, Italy, United States, Japan, Morocco, France, United Kingdom, and Canada.
3. Benjamin Franklin takes a few steps.
4. Benjamin Franklin and Mark Twain.
5. El Rio del Tiempo (The River of Time).
6. The San Angel Inn.
7. Maelstrom.
8. Alfredo's restaurant, and the statue is of Neptune.
9. Venice and the Doge's Palace.
10. The 360-degree film is known as *Wonders of China,* and the narrator is the legendary poet Li Bai.
11. The shrine is a reproduction of the one that can be found at Hiroshima Bay.
12. Japan's Teppanyaki Dining Rooms, sponsored by Mitsukoshi.
13. Morocco.
14. Paris.
15. The movie is *Impressions de France.*
16. The Rose and Crown.
17. The 360-degree film is known as *O Canada!*
18. Canada has a replica of this famous hotel.
19. Between France and the United Kingdom.
20. IllumiNations.

Disney/MGM Studios
Theme Park

·······································

Questions

1. The Studio's landmark is the "Earffel Tower," a pair of Mickey Mouse ears situated atop a water tower. What hat size is that particular pair of Mickey Mouse ears?

2. What is the name of the main street at the Disney/MGM Studios?

3. The Chinese Theatre is home to what popular attraction?

4. What famous pair of slippers are on display in the Chinese Theatre?

5. What company sponsors the Superstar Television attraction?

6. What is the name of the lake at Lakeside Circle?

7. What is the name of the restaurant where almost every table has its very own television set and guests view a series of old television shows?

8. What restaurant is named after a famous Hollywood eating establishment? The restaurant was also in the feature *Fun and Fancy Free* (1947).

9. What is the name of the dinosaur in which you can get "The Ice Cream of Extinction" over at Lakeside Circle?

10. What is your destination on Star Tours, and who are your two pilots?

11. Who are your hosts for The Magic of Disney Animation attraction?

12. What popular Disney action film was made into an attraction in December of 1990?

13. What is the name of the film starring Kermit, Miss Piggy, and the gang?

14. The facade of Mickey's of Hollywood is modeled after what famous Hollywood store?

15. What is the name of the restaurant that places guests in fifties' automobiles and shows science-fiction movies while they enjoy their meals?

Disney/MGM Studios Theme Park

·····································

Answers

1. The "Earffel Tower" is said to wear a size 342 3/8.
2. Hollywood Blvd.
3. The Great Movie Ride.
4. The ruby slippers worn by Judy Garland in *The Wizard of Oz.*
5. Sony is your host for Superstar Television. Sony also sponsors The Great Monster Sound Show at the Disney/MGM Studios with your hosts Martin Short and Chevy Chase.
6. Echo Lake.
7. The 50s Prime Time Cafe.
8. The Hollywood Brown Derby.
9. Gertie, a cartoon character of the early 1900s drawn by Winsor McCay.
10. The destination is the Moon of Endor. Your two pilots are R2-D2 and RX-24, or Rex for short, who is voiced by Paul Reubens.
11. Robin Williams and Walter Cronkite.
12. The *Honey I Shrunk the Kids* Movie Set Adventure.
13. "Muppet Vision 3-D."
14. Frederick's of Hollywood.
15. The Sci-Fi Diner.

Resorts/
Other Attractions

Questions

1. In 1988 The Disney Company purchased the Disneyland Hotel from Wrather Properties and at the same time took over operation of what other two attractions?
2. How did Disneyland establish a direct transportation link with the Disneyland Hotel, providing door-to-door service for the hotel guests in 1961?
3. If one wanted to send a letter to Walt Disney World, what city should appear in the mailing address?
4. What is the fourth floor of the Contemporary Resort Hotel called?
5. Name the waterways that link the Magic Kingdom to some of the Walt Disney World Resorts.
6. Back in 1973 the Golf Resort at Walt Disney World opened its doors, but in 1985 the name of the resort was changed. What is the current name of the Golf Resort?
7. Who is the star of the Electrical Water Pageant?
8. What is the name of the ranch located at Fort Wilderness?
9. Who is *The Empress Lilly* at the Disney Village Marketplace named after?
10. What restaurant at The Grand Floridian is notable because all the service personnel have the same names?
11. What is celebrated every night at Pleasure Island?
12. Where can you find Big Bertha?
13. Where can one find Ariel's Restaurant?
14. What is the largest water slide at Typhoon Lagoon?
15. What is and where can you find the *Miss Tilly*?

Resorts/ Other Attractions

....

Answers

1. The *Queen Mary* and the *Spruce Goose*. The Disney operation of these attractions is due to end in 1992.
2. Disneyland's monorail system was extended to the hotel.
3. Lake Buena Vista, Florida.
4. The Grand Canyon Concourse.
5. The Seven Seas Lagoon and Bay Lake.
6. The current name for the Golf Resort is The Disney Inn.
7. King Neptune.
8. The Tri-Circle D Ranch.
9. *The Empress Lilly* was named in honor of Walt Disney's wife, Lillian.
10. Victoria and Albert's is the restaurant, and all the waiters are named Albert and the waitresses Victoria.
11. A New Year's Eve celebration takes place every night at Pleasure Island.
12. In the Grand Floridian Beach Resort; she's the band organ at the 1900 Park Fare Restaurant.
13. Ariel's Restaurant is located at The Beach Club Resort.
14. Humunga Kowabunga.
15. The *Miss Tilly* is the shipwrecked boat at the top of Mount Mayday at Typhoon Lagoon.

Euro Disney

Questions

1. In what country is the Euro Disney Resort located?
2. What country came in second in the bidding war for Euro Disney?
3. What edifice at the entrance to the theme park at the Euro Disney Resort differentiates it from its American cousins?
4. What is Le Château de la Belle au Bois Dormant?
5. What are the names of the two riverboats that sail the Rivers of the Far West at Euro Disneyland?
6. Euro Disneyland's version of the Haunted Mansion is known as what?
7. Disneyland and the Walt Disney World Magic Kingdom have Tomorrowland. What is the equivalent at Euro Disney?
8. What new park does the Disney organization plan to build adjacent to Euro Disneyland?
9. What Disney relative gave a speech for the opening of Euro Disneyland?

Euro Disney

1. France, northeast of Paris.
2. Spain.
3. Euro Disney has a hotel, The Disneyland Hotel, right at the entrance to the park.
4. The long name quite simply means Sleeping Beauty Castle.
5. The *Mark Twain* and *Molly Brown*.
6. Phantom Manor.
7. Discoveryland, an eighteenth-century Jules Verne view of the future.
8. A Disney/MGM Studios Theme Park.
9. Roy E. Disney, son of Roy O. Disney, Walt's brother and business partner of more than forty years.

Walt Disney and His Legacy

Questions

1. Where was Walt Disney born?
2. What were the names of Walt Disney's mother and father?
3. For over forty years Walt and his older brother Roy were business partners. They began their business in the back half of a real estate office in Los Angeles, California, and later built the studios we know today in Burbank, California. Walt also had two other brothers and a sister. Can you name them?
4. When Walt Disney was nine years old, the Disney family moved to Kansas City. Walt convinced his father to send him to an art school. What was the name of that school?

5. In Kansas City, Walt's father purchased a newspaper delivery business and recruited his sons to help him. Can you name the paper they delivered?

6. Walt Disney's father was born in what country?

7. Before moving with his family from Kansas City to Chicago, Walt Disney held what summer job?

8. How many years of high school did Walt Disney complete?

9. Why did Walt Disney carry a .38 caliber gun during the summer of 1918?

10. In 1918 Walt Disney's attention turned toward World War I; his brother Roy was already in the Navy and his brother Raymond was in the Army. Walt wanted to enlist, but he was too young. How did Walt eventually serve his country?

11. After spending nine months in France, Walt returned to Kansas City. What job did he hold?

12. While working for his first employer, Walt decided to form his own company with a friend named Ub Iwerks, who was also an artist. What was the name of their business?

13. Walt's first attempt at his own company was short-lived. He formed another company that sold advertisements and cartoons to local theaters. What was this second business venture known as?

14. Walt's Kansas City company made modernized versions of fairy tales. Can you name one of the titles?

15. By 1923 the Kansas City market had basically dried up, and Walt realized that if he wanted a future in the movie business, he would have to move to Hollywood. But first Walt was under contract to make a production for a local dentist. Can you name the title of that production?

16. What was the name of the company Walt and his brother Roy formed on October 16, 1923, in California?

17. What was the first series produced at the brothers' new studio, and what did Walt use as his inspiration for the series?

18. What little girl starred with cartoon animals in Walt Disney's first series?

19. Walt's first-named character was a cat in the Alice Comedies. What was its name?

20. For over three years the first series was a moderate success. Then a new character was developed. What was this Lucky Rabbit's name?

21. Who married first, Walt or his brother Roy Disney?

22. Whom did Walt Disney marry, and where did he meet his new wife?
23. In what state was Walt Disney married?
24. Where did the studios move to in 1926, and what was the name of the company changed to?
25. What was the title of the first Mickey Mouse cartoon, and where and when was this released?
26. What made Walt's first Mickey Mouse cartoon so distinctive?
27. Where did Walt Disney go to record the soundtrack for his first Mickey Mouse cartoon?
28. After a year of making Mickey Mouse cartoons, Walt decided to start a new cartoon series with musical themes playing a more important role than the comedy action of the Mickey Mouse films. What was this new series called?
29. What was the first cartoon utilizing this new format of music and animation?
30. What film earned Walt Disney his first Academy Award?
31. Why did Walt Disney win an honorary Academy Award in 1932?

32. What Disney animator was instrumental in convincing Walt Disney to form the Disney Art School on November 15, 1932?

33. At the Disney Studios, what were the "sweatboxes"?

34. In 1935 what international organization honored Walt Disney for his creation of Mickey Mouse?

35. In 1935 who used Mickey Mouse cartoons to help test their new television sets?

36. What was considered the Walt Disney Studio's first hit song?

37. How many children did Walt Disney have?

38. What planned feature was originally referred to as "Disney's folly" because the press said that the concept would never work?

39. What was the title of the first feature to have a soundtrack record album produced from it?

40. During World War II the State Department sent Walt Disney on a goodwill tour to what continent?

41. What was the first year in which Walt Disney released two full-length animated feature productions?

42. When did the Walt Disney Studios move to their current home on Buena Vista Street in Burbank, California?

43. In what year was the first public offering of Walt Disney Productions stock?

44. What feature originally used the slogan "Hear the Picture, See the Music" for its promotional release?

45. Who moved into the Disney Studios in Burbank on December 7, 1941?

46. In 1942 the film industry honored Walt with their highest award, recognizing his consistent high-quality productions. Can you name this award?

47. Beginning in 1948, and for the next decade, Walt Disney made thirteen True-Life Adventure films. How many of these were given Academy Awards?

48. What was Walt Disney's first True-Life Adventure film?

49. In the 1950s Walt referred to a certain group as his "Nine Old Men." What did they do, and where did he get that designation?

50. A spin-off from the True-Life Adventure series was the People and Places series. Can you name the first film?

51. The Buena Vista Distribution Company was formed in 1953 to handle the release of future Disney productions. What was its first release?

52. Immediately prior to the establishment of the Buena Vista Distribution Company, what movie company handled the release of the Disney films?
53. In what capacity was Walt Disney regularly seen on television?
54. Other than the True-Life Adventure and People and Places films, what was the first live-action Disney feature to win an Academy Award?
55. What was the original name suggested for Disneyland, and where was it to be built?
56. What was the name of the company formed by Walt Disney in 1952 to develop his concepts for a theme park?
57. What was the name of the one-eighth-scale model railroad Walt Disney built around his home in Holmby Hills, California?
58. What was the name of the musical band formed by some of the Disney animators, led by Ward Kimball?
59. How old was Walt Disney when Disneyland opened?
60. At what age child did Walt Disney aim his Disneyland park?
61. What Disney live-action production featured a cameo performance by Walt's youngest daughter?
62. Walt Disney received Academy Awards for what two live-action featurettes in 1958 and 1959?
63. Who wrote the first biography of Walt Disney?
64. Where is the first school named after Walt Disney?
65. What live-action Disney production featured a cameo appearance by Walt's grandson, Walter Elias Disney Miller?
66. Walt Disney was asked to provide the pageantry for which Winter Olympic Games?
67. Walt Disney was instrumental in founding what school to train artists and musicians?
68. What award did Walt Disney receive on September 14, 1964, from President Lyndon B. Johnson?
69. Walt Disney created four attractions for what World's Fair?
70. What is the only attraction that has been taken out of Disneyland and relocated in a non-Disney location?
71. What two authors wrote books entitled *The Art of Walt Disney*, more than two decades apart?
72. Walt Disney served as Grand Marshal of what major parade in 1966?
73. In 1966 the National Association of Theatre Owners honored Walt Disney with what special award?
74. How many Academy Awards did Walt Disney receive personally?

75. Which production is the only one that gives a story screen credit to Walt Disney?
76. What are the last animated and live-action features on which Walt Disney worked?
77. How old was Walt Disney when he died?
78. What was the code name Walt Disney used for his Florida Project?
79. What did Walt Disney consider his "greatest gift to mankind"?
80. When Walt Disney died, who took over for him as head of Walt Disney Productions?
81. The 1968 United States postage stamp honoring Walt Disney was issued in what town?
82. When were the Walt Disney Archives established at the Walt Disney Studios to collect and preserve the history of Walt Disney and his company?
83. When did Roy O. Disney die?
84. In 1984 Walt Disney Productions formed a new movie label that would identify films meant to appeal to more mature audiences. Can you name the label and the first film that was released?
85. On September 22, 1984, who became Chairman and Chief Executive Officer of Walt Disney Productions?
86. What is the current name of Walt Disney Productions?
87. In the 1980s Walt Disney Productions made two films in conjunction with Paramount. Can you name them?
88. In what year did the first international Disney park open, and what is its name?
89. Which is the only Disney park in which The Walt Disney Company does not have an ownership interest?
90. What Disney animated feature is the only one to have a PG rating?
91. When did the first Disney Store open, and where is it located?
92. When were the first Disney Dollars produced, and who is featured on the one-, five-, and ten-dollar bills?
93. Other business firms refer to them as customers and employees, but to Disney people what are they referred to as?
94. Who became the first recipient of The Disney Legends Award? This award recognizes significant contributions that have been made over the years by Disney personalities and employees.
95. Where did the first international Disney Store open its doors?

96. What is " Микки Маус "?

97. Where can you find a building that features statues of the Seven Dwarfs supporting the roof, and a building containing the world's largest sundial?

98. What is the name of the third movie division Disney formed in 1990, and what was its first release?

99. What is the name for the planned Anaheim Project, a new theme park to be adjacent to Disneyland, similar to EPCOT Center?

100. What is the name of the new town planned to be built adjacent to Walt Disney World? It is expected to contain some eight thousand new housing units, a medical facility, a Disney school, and an environmental center.

Walt Disney and His Legacy

1. Walter Elias Disney was born on December 5, 1901, at 1249 Tripp Avenue in Chicago, Illinois.
2. Before she married Elias Disney, Walt Disney's mother's name was Flora Call.
3. Herbert was the oldest and became a postman; Raymond was an insurance agent; and sister Ruth moved to Portland, Oregon.
4. Walt Disney attended the Kansas City Art Institute.
5. The Kansas City morning *Times* and the evening and Sunday *Star*.
6. Elias Disney was born in Canada of Irish parents; he moved to the United States when he was a young man.
7. Walt Disney was a news butcher (selling newspapers, candy, and sodas) for the Van Noyes Interstate News Company on the Atchison, Topeka and Santa Fe Railroad.
8. Walt attended only one year of high school at McKinley in Chicago, but he was a self-educated man. His inquisitive mind was always searching for answers, and he retained the knowledge that he sought.
9. Walt carried a .38 caliber gun because he worked as a security guard in Chicago.
10. Walt Disney doctored his passport application to raise his age and joined the American Ambulance Corps, a division of the Red Cross, and was sent to France.
11. He worked as an artist for the Pesmen-Rubin Commercial Art Studio and later for the Kansas City Film Ad Co., which sold advertisements to movie theaters.
12. The company was known as Iwerks-Disney Commercial Artists. The title was originally Disney-Iwerks, but since his partner's name is pronounced "eye-works," Walt said that it sounded too much like an eye doctor's office.
13. The second business venture was incorporated as Laugh-O-gram Films.
14. The series of Laugh-O-grams included "Little Red Riding

Hood, "The Four Musicians of Bremen," "Goldie Locks and the Three Bears," "Jack and the Beanstalk," "Cinderella," and "Puss in Boots."

15. The production was done for the dentist Dr. Thomas B. McCrum, and it was entitled *Tommy Tucker's Tooth*. A few years later Walt made a sequel for the same dentist called *Clara Cleans Her Teeth.*

16. The Disney Bros. Cartoon Studio.

17. The first contract was signed with Margaret J. Winkler for a series called the Alice Comedies. Walt had often given credit for the inspiration for the Alice Comedies to the pioneering animator Max Fleischer and his *Out of the Inkwell* cartoons.

18. Virginia Davis was the first live star of Walt Disney's Alice Comedies. She starred in the pilot film in Kansas City, and later traveled to Hollywood with her family to continue the series.

19. Julius was the cat who aided Alice in the Alice Comedies.

20. The new character was known as Oswald the Lucky Rabbit. The series was less complicated than the Alice Comedies which had used a combination of animation and live-action.

21. Roy and Walt were rooming together until Roy married his childhood sweetheart from Kansas City, Edna Francis, and moved out. That convinced Walt that he should marry, too, which he did three months later.

22. Walt Disney married Lillian Bounds on July 13, 1925. Lillian worked at the Disney Bros. Studio as a secretary.

23. Walt Disney's wife-to-be, Lillian Bounds, was from Idaho, so the couple traveled there to be married (in Lewiston).

24. In May of 1926, Walt moved to a new studio he had built on Hyperion Avenue, and the name was changed to Walt Disney Studios. The name change was Roy's request; he felt that since Walt was the creative one, his name should be on the studio.

25. The very first Mickey Mouse cartoon released was *Steamboat Willie* on November 18, 1928, at the Colony Theatre in New York City at twelve noon. This date is now regarded as Mickey Mouse's official birthday. Two cartoons, *Plane Crazy* and *Gallopin' Gaucho* were completed prior to *Steamboat Willie,* but they were both originally made as silent films, and Walt had been unable to interest theaters in showing them.

26. It featured synchronized sound.

27. New York City.
28. The new series utilizing animation and music was known as Walt Disney's Silly Symphonies.
29. The first Silly Symphony was released under the byline, "Mickey Mouse Presents a Walt Disney Silly Symphony" and was titled *The Skeleton Dance*. It was released in 1929 at the Carthay Circle Theatre in Hollywood, California. Eight years later, Walt premiered his first full-length feature, *Snow White and the Seven Dwarfs* at the same theater.
30. On November 18, 1932, Walt Disney received his first Academy Award for his release of the first full-color cartoon, the Silly Symphony *Flowers and Trees*. The Silly Symphonies became extremely successful, and Walt won the Academy Award each year for the rest of the decade. *Three Little Pigs, The Tortoise and the Hare, Three Orphan Kittens, Country Cousin, The Old Mill, Ferdinand the Bull,* and *The Ugly Duckling* all won Academy Awards.
31. Walt Disney received an Oscar in 1932 for the creation of Mickey Mouse.
32. The Disney animator Art Babbitt suggested the training classes. Walt Disney liked the idea because he could now train and instruct his own animators without having to send them away to school.
33. "Sweatboxes" were the small, poorly ventilated projection rooms at the Disney Studios. The name also was very appropriate because the apprehensive animators showed their pencil tests to Walt there, realizing that a career could be made or lost based on the success of the test.
34. The League of Nations honored Walt in Paris, 1935.
35. RCA used Mickey Mouse cartoons to test their television sets.
36. The first hit song was Frank Churchill's "Who's Afraid of the Big Bad Wolf?" for the 1933 Silly Symphony *Three Little Pigs*. It came in the depths of the Depression, when most Americans were trying to keep the "wolf" away from their doors.
37. The Disneys had two daughters: Diane Marie, born December 18, 1933, and Sharon Mae, born on December 31, 1936.
38. Disney's folly was *Snow White and the Seven Dwarfs*.
39. *Snow White and the Seven Dwarfs* was the first film whose record album was created directly from the film's soundtrack.
40. South America.
41. The year was 1940, and the two full-length feature animated

releases were *Pinocchio* in February and *Fantasia* in November.

42. The move took place over New Year's 1940.

43. The first public offering of Disney stock was made in April of 1940. Some 600,000 shares of common and 150,000 shares of preferred were issued, raising much-needed capital for Walt Disney Productions.

44. "Hear the Picture, See the Music" was used to promote the November 13, 1940, release of *Fantasia*. Another slogan was "Fantasia will Amazia."

45. On December 7, 1941, the Army moved onto the Disney Studio lot, storing ammunition under the parking sheds and setting up a truck-repair facility on the soundstage.

46. In 1942 the Academy of Motion Picture Arts and Sciences honored Walt Disney with the Irving G. Thalberg Award.

47. Walt Disney received eight Academy Awards for his True-Life Adventure documentaries.

48. Against the advice of his distributor, Walt Disney made and released *Seal Island,* which proved itself by winning an Academy Award.

49. The legendary Disney "Nine Old Men" were Walt's top animators: Les Clark, Ward Kimball, Ollie Johnston, Frank Thomas, Marc Davis, Milt Kahl, Woolie Reitherman, Eric Larson, and John Lounsbery. President Roosevelt referred to the Supreme Court as his "Nine Old Men," and Walt reasoned that he had a similar group.

50. The first People and Places film was *The Alaskan Eskimo.* It won an Academy Award in 1953 for Short Subject Documentary. The series continued until 1960. During its close to eight-year run, it captured two other Academy Awards— in 1955 for *Men Against the Arctic* and in 1958 for *Ama Girls.*

51. The first productions handled by the Buena Vista Distribution Company were the 1953 releases of *The Living Desert* and a featurette, *Ben and Me.*

52. Disney films had been released by RKO.

53. From 1954 until his death, Walt Disney was the host of his weekly evening television show (first called *Disneyland,* then *Walt Disney Presents,* and then *Walt Disney's Wonderful World of Color*).

54. The live-action classic *20,000 Leagues Under the Sea* (1954) won two Academy Awards, one for Best Special Effects and the other for Best Art/Set Direction.

55. In 1948 the theme park was called Mickey Mouse Park, and

it was going to be located across the street from the Disney Studios on Riverside Drive.

56. The new company became WED Enterprises, using Walt's initials. In 1986 the name was changed to Walt Disney Imagineering.

57. The Carolwood Pacific. It had an engine that Walt Disney named the *Lilly Belle* in honor of his wife Lillian.

58. They gained fame as the Firehouse Five Plus Two, playing Dixieland jazz.

59. Walt Disney was fifty-three years old when Disneyland opened.

60. A trick question! Walt Disney professed that he was not creating a kiddy park; it was for families. He wanted a place where adults and children could go and have fun together.

61. Walt Disney's daughter Sharon Mae Disney made her cameo appearance in the 1957 release of *Johnny Tremain.*

62. *The Wetback Hound* of 1957 and *Grand Canyon* of 1958.

63. The first biography of Walt Disney was written by his daughter Diane Disney Miller.

64. The first school honoring Walt Disney was dedicated in September 1955, in Tullytown, Pennsylvania. It is known as the Walt Disney Elementary School. Later Walt Disney schools were in towns more closely associated with his life: Marceline, Anaheim, and Burbank.

65. Walter Elias Disney Miller, the fifth child born to Diane Disney and Ron Miller, appeared in the 1963 live-action production *Son of Flubber,* the sequel to *The Absent-Minded Professor* (1961).

66. Walt Disney provided the pageantry for the 1960 Winter Olympic Games in Squaw Valley, California.

67. Walt Disney focused his efforts late in life on helping to establish the California Institute of the Arts, formed by combining the venerable Chouinard Art Institute with the Los Angeles Conservatory of Music.

68. The highest award to any civilian, The Presidential Medal of Freedom, was presented to him, ironically by a president who never paid a visit to Disneyland.

69. The New York World's Fair (1964–65) provided the testing ground for Walt Disney for four attractions that he later moved to Disneyland.

70. Midget Autopia was presented to Marceline, Missouri, in 1966. Walt often said Marceline, where he spent his childhood, provided the inspiration for Main Street, USA.

71. The two authors were Robert Feild and Christopher Finch.

72. The Tournament of Roses Parade in Pasadena, California, picked Walt Disney to lead their New Year's parade in 1966.

73. The Theatre Owners presented Walt Disney with The Showman of the World award.

74. Walt Disney won thirty-two Academy Awards, way more than anyone else. Cedric Gibbons, the art director, is second with eleven Academy Awards.

75. The only time Walt Disney ever received a story screen credit was for the 1965 release *Lt. Robin Crusoe, USN* starring Dick Van Dyke. His name, however, appears backwards in those credits: "Retlaw Yensid."

76. The last features to have that Disney touch were the 1967 releases of *The Jungle Book* and *The Happiest Millionaire*.

77. Walt Disney was just ten days past his sixty-fifth birthday when he passed away on December 15, 1966.

78. Project X. Also known as Project Winter, Project Future, and Project Florida.

79. Walt Disney referred to his EPCOT project as his greatest gift to mankind.

80. When Walt Disney passed away on December 15, 1966, from an acute circulatory collapse resulting from lung cancer, the natural choice to replace him at that time was his brother, Roy Disney.

81. Marceline, Missouri, was chosen as the "first day of issue" town for the Walt Disney stamp because of the time that Walt had spent there as a child.

82. The Disney Archives opened its doors in 1970.

83. Roy died just three months after the dedication of Walt Disney World, on December 20, 1971. One cannot underestimate the importance of Roy O. Disney; his financial savvy kept the company above water through many tough years, and he provided the needed support when the company was ready to grow.

84. The new movie division was Touchstone, and the first release was *Splash*.

85. Michael Eisner became Chairman and Chief Executive Officer. Frank Wells also became President and Chief Operating Officer on the same day.

86. On February 11, 1986, Walt Disney Productions changed its name to The Walt Disney Company.

87. The joint efforts were *Popeye* in 1980 and *Dragonslayer* in 1981.

88. Tokyo Disneyland opened on April 15, 1983, on a section of landfill in Tokyo Bay.

89. Tokyo Disneyland. The park is owned by the Oriental Land Company, a Japanese concern, who runs it under license from The Walt Disney Company.

90. The only PG-rated animated feature was *The Black Cauldron* (1985).

91. The first Disney Store was opened March 28, 1987, in Glendale, California.

92. The first Disney Dollars were produced in 1987, and featured on the one is Mickey, on the five, Goofy, and on the ten, Minnie.

93. For Disney people, customers are referred to as "guests" and employees are considered "cast members."

94. The first recipient of the Disney Legends Award was Fred MacMurray, who placed his handprints in cement at the Disney Studios in 1987.

95. The first international Disney Store opened on November 1, 1990, on Regent Street in London, England.

96. " Микки Маус " is Mickey Mouse in Russian, and he first appeared in a Russian comic book in July 1990.

97. Both are Team Disney buildings. The Seven Dwarfs support the roof of the Disney Studio's Team Disney building in California, and the world's largest sundial is in the Team Disney building at the Walt Disney World resort in Florida.

98. The third movie company is known as Hollywood Pictures; its first release was *Arachnophobia.*

99. The new theme park adjacent to Disneyland is to be known as WESTCOT Center.

100. This Disney type of town is to be called Celebration, and it will open its doors sometime after the year 2000.

As you may have noticed, this book
does contain a total of 999 questions.
And, just like the Haunted Mansion that claims
to house 999 happy haunts, where there is always
room for one more ghost, there is also always
room for one more trivia question.